FLAK AND BARBED WIRE

'IN THE WAKE OF WUPPERTAL'

GORDON STOOKE

Published in Australia – 1997
by AUSTRALIAN MILITARY HISTORY PUBLICATIONS.
13 Veronica Place, Loftus, 2232, Australia.
Phone: 015 284 760 or (02) 9521 6515.

Written by GORDON STOOKE.

Printed by:
P. S. Print, Kirrawee, NSW.

Artwork by:
Peninsular Grafics, Caringbah, NSW.

Typesetting in Times Roman 10.5pt by:
Typesmith, South Hurstville, NSW.

Proofreader: Alan Lannan

National Library of Australia, NSW
ISBN: 0-9586693-2-5

Action Photographs by courtesy of
RAAF Museum, Point Cook, Victoria.

To my crew,
ever confident,

and

To my wife for her
encouragement and patience

ETERNALLY GRATEFUL:

Paolo Smeyers and Yannick Bruynoghe

THANK YOU:

Paolo and Jeannie Smeyers, Binche, Belgium.
Marie-Claire Deflandre-Nicod, Arbre, Belgium.
Jacques Mason, Paris, France.
Luc Smolders, Alken, Belgium.
Jean-Louis Roba, Charleroi, Belgium.
Valda and Don Tibbits, Melbourne, Australia.
Brian and Helen Morris, Melbourne, Australia.
Malcolm Jeffrey, Australian Plastic Card Co. Pty. Ltd.
Robina Norton, Melbourne, Australia.
Jack Eggleton, Melbourne, Australia.

CONTENTS

LIST OF MAPS AND PHOTOGRAPHS

LIST OF MAPS AND PHOTOGRAPHS continued

PAGE

FOREWORD

This absorbing story by Gordon Stooke, held my intense interest from the first chapter through to the epilogue. I am sure all who survived in the Allied Air Forces during World War 11 (particularly Bomber Command) will be similarly affected. Also those airmen who were the "Guests" of the Germans and their relatives, will find it difficult to put this book down.

Personally I found great empathy with Gordon as we have much in common. We are both survivers from dramatic parachute jumps and were fortunate to complete our squadrons motto "Strike and Return", even though it took Gordon 45 years to make it back to Binbrook.

It is even possible that I selected him for pilot training in 1941.

I was proud to be posted to command 460 Squadron in 1944 and later that year to take command of R.A.F. Station Binbrook.

It was on my tenth trip to Germany that I too had to bail out at a very low altitude after colliding with another Lancaster in the middle of the night at 10,000 feet. My aircraft lost its port wing and went into an uncontrollable spin. I was more fortunate than Gordon because I landed in Allied occupied territory. Although listed as missing at Binbrook, I was able to return to England a week later. By strange coincidence the replacement Lancaster I had arranged to pick up at Northolt airfield near London, was "P" for Peter, the same letter as the aircraft I had lost.

In Gordon's book he mentions the risk aircrew had to take. Let me emphasize that only 3% of the men who enlisted during World War 11 were trained as aircrew and posted to the U.K. or the Middle East, yet from this small group 39% of all Australian casualties occurred, with 1000 of them coming from 460 Squadron.

Truly they were the front line troops of the war and bore the brunt of our sacrifice. Even whilst I was in command at Binbrook, the losses were not nearly as severe or as drastic as in 1942/3, when Gordon flew. Even so, I knew that of every three crews that arrived at the Squadron, one would be lost within two or three weeks.

These physically perfect, intelligent young men, possessed with will power and determination to press on regardless, were the elite of Australian youth who not only maintained but enhanced the reputation of Australia and its people.

Gordon Stooke is one of these men and whilst he never claims to be heroic, he certainly is one who helped to ensure the freedom we enjoy today. This story is worth reading and storing in our archives for all time.

Keith Parsons,
5th May, 1996

Air Commodore K. R. Parsons, C.B.E., D.S.O., D.F.C., A.F.C.

PREFACE

Even though the events in this story took place a long time ago, they are still vivid in my memory. Perhaps the setting down of these experiences may help me to exorcise the effects of some of them.

My story is not unique - during 1939/45 thousands of other youngsters found themselves thrust into situations for which they were not, nor could have been, prepared. On behalf of those who survived and the many who did not, I offer this account of what happened to one airman who came to grief over Europe.

It is not my intention to become dreary or melancholy in the telling of my story. Nevertheless it is important for readers to understand the almost "no-win" circumstances under which aircrew operated in Bomber Command.

During 1943/44, night raids by R.A.F. Bomber Command increased in frequency and intensity. At the same time, so did the effectiveness of the German defences. Night fighters used sophisticated radar tracking devices to find bombers in the dark and the aim of predicted anti-aircraft guns and searchlights, was unerring. Even though German location techniques were countered to some extent by radar disrupting devices and other measures, the inevitable result was an ever increasing toll on British aircrew and aircraft.

Maximum Effort raids on German targets such as the Ruhr Valley, Hamburg, Nuremburg, Munich and Berlin by Lancasters, Halifaxes, Stirlings and Wellingtons, on occasions included as many as 1000 aircraft. Usually though, approximately 750 R.A.F. bombers were deployed. Losses, sometimes higher than 10% of each raid (eg. Berlin), averaged 35 aircraft or 245 aircrew per raid. Only 10% of those lost were reported as becoming prisoners-of-war.

Competence, experience or just plain luck. Those of us who survived Bomber Command must have been sponsored by at least one of these guardian angels. To be involved in a theatre of war where your chance of survival was an official and I believe, conservative 14%, was grim, to say the least. It can be shown that 75% of those lost had completed less than 15 of their required tour of 30 operations, so experience was certainly a life-saving factor. Those who did survive 1943/44, are walking miracles and I give thanks to providence that I am a member of a complete surviving aircrew.

How did aircrew maintain morale in the face of such unacceptable odds? Possibly it was because they were all so young and with the optimism of youth, never believing "it" would happen to them. Infallible youth? Overconfidence? Pride? Maybe all shut their minds to reality when exposed to constant danger. Even under the most adverse circumstances, few were willing to dwell on the possibility that they might lose their lives. While over enemy territory they were too busy. Only later after the danger had passed, did a nervous witticism or two, or possibly fake bravado reveal unexpressed fears and mute relief.

Even the loss of comrades was accepted as part of the game. I lost my close boyhood friend, Ken Evans, to Bomber Command but I felt his loss so much more when I returned home and he did not, than I did in February 1944 when I heard that Ken had been shot down.

In a sad, paradoxical way, I suppose, with sword in hand we came to accept mates 'getting the chop' as part of life in those irrational and dispassionate days.

GORDON STOOKE 1945.

GLOSSARY OF TERMS

ABWEHR – German counter-espionage service.

ASTRODOME – Bubble on top of aircraft for star sighting.

AVRO ANSEN – Two engine training aircraft.

B17 – American heavy bomber.

BF110 – German fighter/bomber.

'BIPLANE' – The Binbrook radio callsign.

BLITZKREIG – Germany's 'Lightning War'.

'BLOCKADE' – 460 Squadron's radio call sign.

BOSCHE – French derogatory term for Germans.

BOUGHT IT – Killed.

BURTON – Go for a Burton - euphemism for killed.

BUZZ – Fly very low to scare people.

CONED – Caught in a concentration of searchlights.

COOKIE – A 4000 lb T.N.T. bomb in a canister.

CORKSCREW – Twisting manoeuvre to disrupt fighters and gunners.

DAKOTA - DC3 – American designed transport aircraft.

DICKEY – Unsure or unsafe.

DISPERSAL – Aircraft parking areas around an airfield.

DUTY PILOT – Ground controller of aircraft movements.

ERSATZ – German for; a substitute/alternative.

FELDWEBEL – German sergeant.

FLAK – German for; anti-aircraft shell bursts.

FLIGHT – A basic complement of aircraft.

FOCKER TRIPLANE – German WW1 fighter aircraft.

FORM 700 – Pilot's airworthiness acceptance document.

FW190 – German fighter aircraft.

GEHEIMEFELDPOLIZEI – German secret police.

GESTAPO – German State Secret Police.

G.I. – General Issue - euphamism for an American Private.

GROUP – A number of Wings of aircraft.

HALIFAX – British heavy bomber.

HAUPTMANN – German captain.

INTERCOM – Internal aircraft communications system.

JU88 – German fighter/bomber.

KITTYHAWK – American fighter aircraft.

KRIEGYS – Slang for Kriegsgefangene - P.O.W.

LANCASTER – British heavy bomber.

LEBENSRAUM – Living room.

LUFTWAFFE – German air force.

LUGER – German pistol.

MAE WEST – Inflatable life jacket.

MARQUIS – French underground guerillas.

METRO – Paris underground railway.

MOSQUITO – British fighter/bomber.

ME109 – German fighter aircraft.

NACHTJAGER – Night fighter

NAZI – National Socialist Party.

'OBOE' – British radar system.

PANCAKE – Land an aircraft with wheels up.

PATHFINDER – Target-marking aircraft.

PLAYERS – British brand of cigarettes.

P.O.W. – Prisoner of War.

RAAF – Royal Australian Air Force.

RADAR – Radio location system.

RAF – Royal Air Force.

RCAF – Royal Canadian Air Force.

RED BARON – Famous WW1 German fighter ace.

RIP CORD – Parachute release cord.

RUSSKY – Nickname for a Russian soldier.

S.D. – German security service.

SPITFIRE – British fighter aircraft.

SQUADRON – A number of Flights of aircraft.

S.S. – German Army Protection Corps.

STALAG – POW camp.

STEN GUN – British light machine-gun.

THUNDERBOLT – American fighter aircraft.

TIGER MOTH – British trainer aircraft.

TRACER – Self-illuminating bullets.

U.S.A.A.F. – United States of American Air Force.

W.A.A.F. – Womens Auxilary Air Force.

WALLOON – People of southern Belgium (French extract).

WEAVING – see Corkscrewing.

WEHRMACHT – German Regular army.

WELLINGTON – British medium bomber.

WINDOW – Tinfoil dropped to confuse German radar.

WING – A number of squadrons of aircraft.

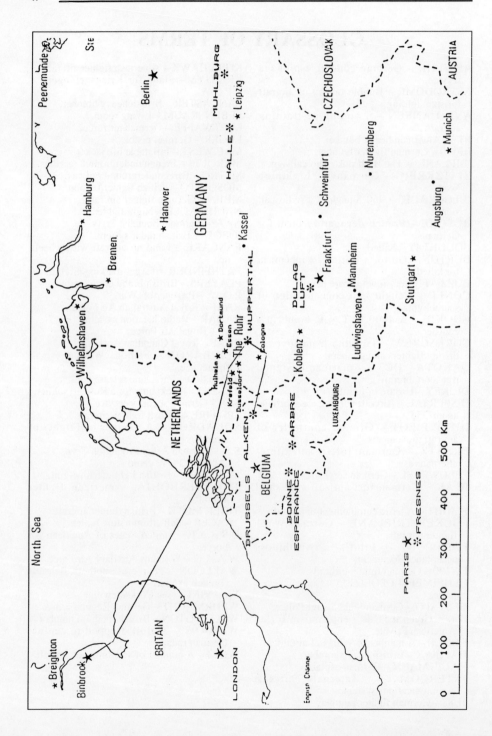

CHAPTER 1

460 SQUADRON -
ROYAL AUSTRALIAN AIR FORCE
(BOMBER COMMAND)

Until the night of June 24, 1943 I had lived an uncomplicated 20 years, 3 months and 15 days. I was about to keep an appointment with destiny.

Like hundreds of other 20 year olds, I was the pilot and captain of a Lancaster four-engined heavy bomber. The target for that night was the German city of Wuppertal in the Ruhr valley. Dusk was falling and with propellers lazily ticking over, my bomb-laden aircraft was one of 15, queued nose to tail, awaiting its turn to take off.

460 squadron was one of five Australian heavy bomber squadrons in Bomber Command and had already achieved a proud record. Even so, by war's end my squadron had flown more sorties (6,264), dropped more bombs (24,856 tons) and received more decorations than any other squadron in the history of the Royal Air Force.

The Ruhr WAS industrial Germany. Nicknamed "Happy Valley", just to be

*THE CREW OF D - DONALD L-R: THE AUTHOR (PILOT), DENNIS TOOHIG
(WIRELESS OPERATOR FROM LONDON), STAN 'ROWDY' NOWLAN (REAR GUNNER
FROM CASINO NSW), NORM CONKLIN (BOMB AIMER FROM SYDNEY NSW),
CLARRIE CRAVEN (NAVIGATOR FROM CANOWINDRA NSW).
NOT PICTURED: COL BROADBENT (ENGINEER FROM LONDON), FRANK SHAW
(MID UPPER GUNNER FROM ADELAIDE), DAN DOWNEY (GUNNER FROM SYDNEY).*

contrary I guess, it included Essen, Dortmund and Duisburg. Close by were Krefeld, Dusseldorf, Wuppertal and Cologne. With the arguable exception of Berlin, it was the most heavily defended area in Germany. Lancasters, Halifaxes, Stirlings and Wellingtons had to withstand constant attacks by hundreds of Luftwaffe Messerschmitt Bf 110s, Junkers Ju 88s and Focke-Wulf Fw 190s nachtjagers (night fighters) in the air, and heavy concentrations of anti-aircraft and searchlight batteries on the ground. In that summer of 1943 most visits to Germany by Bomber Command had been to the Ruhr.

My crew and I had flown together for three months, having teamed up at No.27 Operational Training Unit, in Lichfield, Staffordshire, in January 1943. There we received concentrated aerial warfare training in twin-engined Wellington medium bombers. Later, at No. 1662 Conversion Unit, Blyton, Yorkshire, flying four-engined Halifaxes and Lancasters, we were joined by an Australian Mid-Upper Gunner and an English Engineer.

I felt a heavy responsibility for the lives of these six older men as three were married. It was only their total acceptance of me as their pilot that put my concern somewhat to rest.

Unseasonably bleak winter winds had deposited a blanket of snow on the Yorkshire moors when we arrived at 460 Squadron R.A.A.F., Bomber Command, Breighton, in early May, 1943. With us were two other 'sprog' crews, one skippered by Danny Rees (Conspicuous Gallantry Medal) from Western Australia and the other by Jim Sharp (Distinguished Flying Cross) from New South Wales. Breighton was a temporary wartime aerodrome with cold, draughty Nissen huts for billets and flight offices. Spring rains on snow ensured that commuting between huts and flight offices was both wet and quaggy. I could only imagine what it was like in mid-winter. Maybe it might have been better with the ground frozen solid or perhaps worse! We had only just settled in when Group Captain Hughie Edwards, V.C., D.S.O., D.F.C., announced that the squadron was to move to a permanent R.A.F. station at Binbrook, Lincolnshire.

This we did by air on the 14th May. Horsa Gliders, towed by Albemarle aircraft, transferred 850 personnel and 90 odd tons of 460's equipment. Another 200, plus personal goods and chattels were loaded aboard our Lancasters. I can still see my pushbike's wheels protruding from our bomb bay like auxiliary undercarriage. This prompted comment in the mess at Binbrook that night, with one whit quipping, "Hey, Stooke, don't you trust the undercart provided by Avro?"

Our new 'Peacetime' Station with its comfortable sleeping quarters and substantial mess facilities was pure luxury compared to Breighton. Riding my bicycle from billet to flight offices on made roads instead of muddy dirt tracks, was only one of the many pleasures to be found at a permanent station like Binbrook. The local 'watering hole', the 'Marquis of Granby' in Binbrook village, was a popular diversion, made more so by the compatibility of our hostess, Irene.

Trouble was brewing in the Sergeant's Mess. The pre-installed 'Admin Types' had organised table service and white table-cloths. The newly arrived aircrew, after queuing for their meals, ate on bare benches until a swift protest

AN AVRO LANCASTER IN FLIGHT

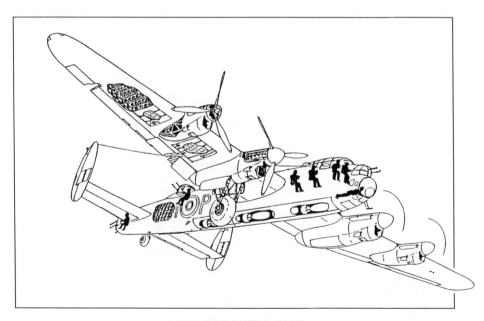

LANCASTER CREW LAYOUT
L-R; REAR GUNNER-MID UPPER GUNNER-RADIO OPERATOR-NAVIGATOR-ENGINEER-
PILOT-BOMB AIMER.

and a hastily convened meeting, soon righted this injustice.

At Binbrook we were allocated Lancaster Mk.1, Serial No: W4320, radio-telephone call sign UV-D-Dog. For personal reasons I always used D-Donald. Nobody ever objected. We had our own aircraft at last!!

The Avro Lancaster was truly a magnificent aircraft and handled like an oversized Avro Anson trainer. Considering its size, it was light on controls, responsive and manoeuvrable. Powered by four Rolls Royce Merlin engines, together producing nearly 6000 horsepower at take off, the Lanc' certainly was a pleasure to fly. Landings were almost "Tiger Moth-ish", the aircraft floating along the runway and your check-check-check back on the control column, producing a perfect three point landing. Well, sometimes!

Its ability to raise massive bomb loads never ceased to amaze, culminating in 1945 when it lifted aloft a monster 10 ton "Grand Slam, Earthquake" bomb, by far the largest and heaviest load ever carried by any aircraft to that time. Surely the mighty Lancaster can be acclaimed as the most effective of all the heavy bombers operating during World War 2.

This wonderful aircraft evolved as a result of redesigning a failure. Designed by Roy Chadwick for A.V. Rowe Ltd., the original Manchester was fitted with twin Rolls Royce Vulture engines, a new type that proved to be a troublesome flop. The Manchester could not carry its designed bombload and was difficult to fly, so Chadwick redesigned the wing and installed four Rolls Royce Merlin engines, creating the mighty Lancaster. Of almost 1,000,000 tons of bombs dropped over Germany by the R.A.F., the Lancaster alone carried 610,000 tons. It is interesting to note that this was in excess of the total dropped on Europe by the United States Air Force.

INCENDIARIES BEING LOADED ONTO D-DONALD
PRIOR TO A RAID ON DUSSELDORF - 25 MAY 1943.

To be fair, the bomb load of the American B17 Flying Fortress was limited because that aircraft had to be very heavily armed to protect itself from constant enemy fighter attacks during daylight raids. The B17 was truly a mighty "Flying Fortress", destroying many thousands of attacking German fighters.

D-Donald's maiden operation over enemy territory was on the 18-19 May, 1943. Our task, along with 12 other Lancasters and 4 Wellingtons was to lay mines in the estuary of the Gironde River, Bordeaux, France.

We took off at dusk and at 6000 feet, crossed the English Channel. Over the French provinces of Normandie, Maine and Poitou, tension grew as, for the first time, we were over enemy occupied territory. We approached the mouth of the Gironde, came down low and prepared to drop our mines.

Suddenly enemy anti-aircraft guns opened up from both sides of the narrow estuary, spraying us with tracers. Two nights previously, Wing Commander Guy Gibson of 617 Dambuster Squadron had a similar experience, albeit considerably more dicey, at the Mohne, Eder and Sorpe Dams. This comparison might well be inappropriate, nevertheless I remember thinking to myself as tracers hosed us and I might even have said it aloud - "Hell, this is bloody dangerous". It was hard to resist the temptation to duck, however futile it might have been.

As tracers passed between wing and tailplane, I heard 'Rowdy' Nowlan exclaim over the intercom, "Hey, careful Skipper". As though I could do anything about it! The Jerry gunners missed and D-Donald was not damaged.

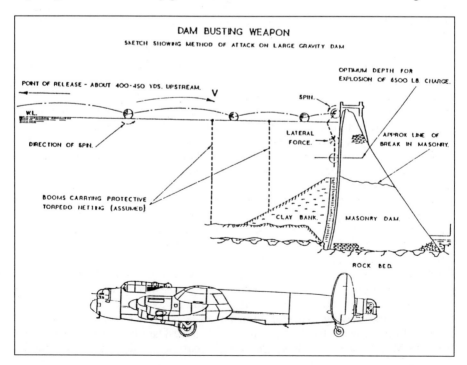

Our initiation into the "Battle of the Ruhr" came on the 23 May, 1943 when we raided Dortmund in "Happy Valley". Unlike our American counterparts, who bombed in daylight and in formation, until mid 1944 R.A.F. Bomber Command attacked only at night, prohibiting formation flying. As up to 1000 bombers were often involved, times and heights over the target were planned so that aircraft approached in waves. This helped reduce the number of collisions with 'friendlies' - a major cause of bomber loss.

More experienced skippers had advised me to corkscrew from the Dutch coast to the target and back again. This, they said, would disrupt both the German radar and the aim of their nightfighter pilots. I did not have to be told twice. Corkscrewing involved turning 15 degrees left and down 100ft, then 30 degrees right and up 200ft. Dan Downey, mid-upper gunner, was continually air sick and eventually had to be replaced by Frank Shaw from Adelaide. For Dan and for the crew, it was most unfortunate but Frank proved to be an excellent replacement. Later the Powers-That-Be argued that corkscrewing caused too many collisions with friendly aircraft, so pilots were discouraged from adopting the practice.

German nightfighters were directed onto British bombers by ground-controlled radar. This was countered by attacking aircraft dropping 'Window' - strips of tinfoil that blurred the radar image of the bombers, rendering the German ground stations ineffective. Ground stations were eventually abandoned and Nazi nightfighters were equipped with onboard radar homing-in devices.The Luftwaffe found this system effective although the use of 'Window' still caused problems. 'Window' was a simple method of disrupting a complicated German detection system.

As we approached Dortmund it was already alight from incendiaries dropped by waves of bombers in front of us. The visual impact was unbelievable, almost abstract. This large city was on fire. Dozens of probing searchlights turned night into day, while down below, thousands of flickering lights pinpointed bomb strikes. In front of us, the smoke balls from hundreds of exploding anti-aircraft shells appeared as an impregnable barrier that had to be flown through.

Over to my right, I saw a bomber caught in a cone of searchlights. Suddenly it exploded and a horrific blood-red fireball attested to the accuracy of the German anti-aircraft gunners and ostentatiously proclaimed the obliteration of another seven brave British airmen.

All seemed to be organised turmoil and you had to be sharp-eyed to carefully pick your way through dozens of other attacking bombers illuminated by fires and searchlights. It was a crazy game of 30-ton dodgem at 20,000 feet.

We managed to fly straight and level long enough to make an accurate bombing run on a cluster of red flares dropped over the aiming point by Pathfinder aircraft. This was a time of concentrated co-operation between bomb-aimer and pilot until "Bombs gone, Photoflash gone" was called. Releasing over 10,000lbs of bombs caused the aircraft to spring up as if in a lift. As we turned for home, corkscrewing, our rear-gunner Rowdy Nowlan saw in the moonlight the vast floods caused by the breaching of Mohne Dam by the Dambusters on the 16th May. When we reached the Dutch coast we could still see Dortmund

DAMAGE TO BERT FURHMANN'S LANCASTER,
AFTER THE RAID ON DORTMUND. 23.5.1943

ablaze 130 miles behind us.

"Hello Biplane, this is Blockade D-Donald, may I land?" With these words I heralded our having 'made it' back to base. We had confirmed our initiation into Bomber Command. It was those words that released the pent-up emotions and unexpressed fear and relief of all seven men aboard D-Donald. We were home safe and after all, tomorrow was another day.

The experience of three operations in quick succession, (Dortmund - record 2000 tons dropped, Dusseldorf - shocking weather, and then Essen), did little to lessen the intense feeling of relief each time we passed back over the English coast. Inside enemy territory we were too preoccupied to be apprehensive. On return, with the pressure off, belief in youthful infallibility might have become somewhat dented.

So it must have been for another 460 Squadron pilot who brought back dead and wounded crewmen from three successive raids. To what extent might his own performance have been affected by the loss of his comrades? Later 'Happy Valley' claimed him and his crew and they were all reported as killed in action.

Each operation had its close shave. On our way to Dusseldorf for example, a Stirling bomber to our left, corkscrewed to the right and up as we corkscrewed to the left and down. Luckily I saw him in the light of the moon and wrenched the control column back hard. I knew we were going to hit. No doubt about it. Intrigued, even strangely unconcerned, I muttered to myself, annoyed. "So this is how you go for a Burton." 'Burton' was an English ale, the saying being an offhanded, unconcerned way of saying - killed.

8

*THE AUTHOR SMILES WITH RELIEF - HAPPY TO ESCAPE RETRIBUTION AFTER
'BUZZING' HESLINGTON HALL.*

We missed!! Near enough, though, to feel a violent jolt of turbulence as the
Stirling passed close beneath us.

Close shaves were not restricted to night-time over Germany. For instance,
Jim Nuttall, our Australian air-frame ground staff corporal, while on leave near
York, had said his goodbyes to a friend, outside a very large house which he
described as "looking like a mansion". As we were scheduled for a night-flying
aircraft test that afternoon, he asked me if he could come with us and try to find
his mansion from the air. I signed the low-flying clearance book (no lower than
500ft) and away we went.

Starting from York, following Jim's instructions, I "drove" the Lancaster
down a large main road at 500ft, until he recognised a street off to the right. I
obediently "turned down" it and sure enough, there was Jim's mansion.

One pass at 500ft brought only two or three people out onto the roof and into
the garden. Not good enough! Two more attacks at flagpole height with our four
Merlins roaring and soon all vantage points were crowded, everyone waving
excitedly. Or so we thought. In fact they were angrily shaking their fists at us, as
I was shortly to find out.

Over the Binbrook runway I called up for permission to land. "Hello Biplane,
this is Blockade D-Donald. May I pancake. Over. "The Air Controller replied,
"Hello Blockade D-Donald, this is Biplane. Pancake. After dispersal, skipper to
report immediately to the duty pilot. Over and out."

When I arrived at the control tower, the duty pilot looked grim. "Were you low-flying anywhere in Yorkshire?" he asked sternly.

"Yes," I said, as there was no point in lying. "But I had a low-flying clearance."

"Did you go lower than 500ft?" A smile flickered across his face.

"Do you think I'd do a thing like that?" I said, evasively.

"Well." He burst out laughing. "Some silly clot has been buzzing Four Group Headquarters in a Lancaster and all the Air Marshals in the R.A.F. are after his blood."

"Not mine, if I can help it," I said, making for the door.

I got out fast because my career in the R.A.A.F could well have ended there and then. One of those who shook his fist at us from the roof of R.A.F. Station Heslington Hall was Air Vice Marshal C. R. Carr, CB, CBE, DFC, AFC. He or one of his staff had seen our aircraft letter, D-Donald but not the squadron letters - UV.

A very angry A.V.M. Carr had personally sent an urgent signal to all Lancaster squadrons in the area, demanding that he immediately be informed of the name, rank and number of the perpetrator pilot.

Our accommodating duty pilot signalled back that it certainly was not one of 460's aircraft. That was another near miss that might have been as effective as a short and accurate cannon burst from a vengeful Luftwaffe nachtjager.

At 1100 hrs on the 27th May the squadron was visited by Their Majesties King George VI and Queen Elizabeth. They were greeted by Air Commodore Rice, Air Officer Commanding No 1 Group and Group Captain Edwards. It was pleasant to be 'close enough to touch'.

That night we raided Essen. The weather was filthy and the target was completely overcast. The Pathfinder marker flares were set to burst above the clouds and Norm Conklin aimed for these. It is interesting to note that we bombed Essen without seeing it.

Leave was allocated on a roster system at 460 Squadron, so on the 7th June, like it or not, I boarded a train at Market Rasen and was on my way to London with a 10 Day pass in my pocket.

Mr. and Mrs. Jack Hewitt had a beautiful home near Hazlemere, Surrey. He was an old friend of my father and took a great interest in my comings and goings whilst I was in England. I suppose he felt he should keep his eye on a young 20 year-old 'undefiled' lad so far from parental guidance.

Anyway I hightailed it to Hazlemere and Mrs. Hewitt picked me up at the station in their little Ford Prefect which struggled up the hill to their home.

I must admit it did me no harm to abandon my uniform, flop into one of Jack Hewitt's big cosy chairs and sip a scotch or two. Through large picture windows I enjoyed the panorama of Hazlemere village with the Surrey countryside as a backdrop. Mrs Hewitt's cooking was pretty good too. I endured this torment for two or three days and then went up to London.

As the next week was of little interest to other than a fellow paragon of sobriety and virtue, it shall remain unrecorded. Suffice to say that on the 15th of June I found myself on the train back to Binbrook.

On the 16th June, 1943, Bomber Command raided Cologne on the Rhine River, south of the Ruhr. We were routed over the Dutch coast between Rotterdam and Antwerp to avoid the anti-aircraft defences set up by the Germans in those otherwise friendly cities.

At about 20,000ft and 5 miles from the coast, we noticed gun flashes from below which we identified as coming from a German flak ship. (Flak - Flugabwehrkanonen - aircraft defence cannon). These boats were just large enough to support a standard German 88mm anti-aircraft gun. We took little notice, as accuracy was not supposed to be one of a flak ship's strong points. Five miles out to sea, they had none of the sophisticated radar tracking devices used ashore. Or so we were told!

Ten minutes later, as I began to corkscrew in earnest, our inter-communication system became unserviceable. As we were now unable to talk to each other, it would have been a bit dicey if we had been attacked by a fighter. Then our starboard outer engine started to heat up and the engineer, Col' Broadbent, feathered it. The mid-upper machine gun turret, operated by a hydraulic pump driven by this engine, was no longer working.

More concerned about the lack of intercom and the mid-upper turret than the feathered starboard engine, I decided that it might be better to go home and live to fight another day. So I aborted the operation and turned back to base.

One of the bombs we carried was nicknamed a "Cookie" - a horrifying missile in the shape of a very large jam tin measuring 8'11" long x 2'7" diameter. 4000lbs of pure T.N.T. was packed inside it. Its purpose was to produce a monstrous blast effect, knocking buildings over. As the cookie was very touchy, we were not allowed to land with one in the bomb bay so I decided to jettison it over the North Sea. With great care!!

What better way then than to do a bombing run on our persistent flak ship still popping away downstairs. A bit like killing a fly with a sledgehammer, you might say. Still it would be good bombing practice. With little to disturb him, Norm Conklin the bomb-aimer was most accurate in his aim. He let the "cookie" go and we waited. It took about a minute. Then the father and mother of all flashes came from the sea below.

Soon we felt heavy turbulence from the shock wave. We never found out how close to the flak ship our "cookie" was when it exploded but if it had landed within a mile or so, it must have sunk her. If not, Herr Kapitan sure would have had a wow of a headache.

During de-briefing back at Binbrook, we claimed one flak ship sunk but were never credited with the kill. We were robbed!!

Wouldn't you know it? At briefing on the 21st June it was announced that the target for tonight was "Happy Valley" again. The fourteenth time in succession for Bomber Command. This time it was Krefeld, north west of Dusseldorf. At least Krefeld was the closest Ruhr city to England. In and out quickly! No problems! Cocky confidence now, it seems.

Just after take off, with the four Merlins roaring as they literally dragged the fully loaded Lancaster into the air, I was shocked to see Corporal Jim Nuttall, our groundstaff airframes man, standing at my right elbow.

*A LANCASTER BOMBER SILHOUETTED BY FIRES AND BOMB AND
ANTI-AIRCRAFT EXPLOSIONS*

*THE SIZE OF A "COOKIE" IS GRAPHICALLY DEMONSTRATED BY THE MAN
SITTING ASTRIDE IT.*

"What the bloody hell are you doing here?" I shouted, hardly able to compete with the screaming engines.

"I just wanted to do one operation - just one," he explained. "I just wanted to find out what it's like".

"You bloody idiot, you'll find out what it's like all right, you'll have us all court-martialled," I yelled. What to do? I could not go back. That would be a disaster for me and for Nuttall, but how could we go on over enemy territory with an extra man aboard?

"Have you got a parachute and an oxygen mask?" I roared furiously.

"I certainly have," said our unauthorised passenger and showed them to me.

"Go back to the astrodome and plug in there." I felt like making him use his parachute there and then, "And make sure you keep out of Dennis's way." The only practical solution was to take 'Nutty' Nuttall with us. After all, what Wing Commander Martin's eyes did not see his heart would not grieve for.

As we climbed up to the rendezvous point, for just a moment I pondered on what the Germans would think of supernumerary Jim, if we were shot down. A spy maybe? Or a saboteur? I pictured Jim with his back to a wall in front of a firing squad. Trouble was I could not tell whether the uniforms were German or British!

There were more pressing problems than Jim Nuttall as the mid-upper turret had gone unserviceable and jammed, so our defences were cut in half. I told Frank to fire his guns anyway if we were attacked. It just might frighten the Jerry pilot away. Ever the optimist!

After we crossed the Dutch coast 'Rowdy' Nowlan reported seeing an Me 110 and then a Fw 190 so I corkscrewed even harder.

It was a clear night and the Pathfinders had done an excellent job. The target was well marked with the more accurate red markers dropped by Mosquito aircraft directed by OBOE target finding system. Plenty of Pathfinder green flares in support too, although we bombed on the red. More searching Jerry fighters were seen on the way out but happily they left us alone.

After we landed back at Binbrook, I got rid of Corporal Nuttall but quick! Later he confided to a mate, "They're all crackpots, the whole bloody lot of them. Anyone who does that more than once, ought to be certified." He was quite right of course.

The target for the night of the 22nd June was Mulheim - the Ruhr Valley again!! Two operations in a row! At this rate I reckoned our tour would be finished in record time; a case of counting my chickens? Mulheim was a medium-sized city tucked in between Duisburg and Essen, just near the junction of the Rhein and the Ruhr rivers. Immediately to the north was Oberhausen, Mulheim's twin city. Four cities so close together added up to a fearful hot-bed of defences. Attacking any one, meant running the gauntlet of the other three heavily defended areas.

I had weaved our way to within two or three miles of the target when suddenly the whole aircraft was blanketed in a blaze of blinding light. Dazzled, I realised that we were 'coned' by searchlights. To be coned meant that after one predicted radar-controlled searchlight caught a bomber in its beam, a dozen or so manually operated searchlights homed in, all beams together forming the shape of a cone with the aircraft clearly visible at the apex. The trapped bomber would then be fired at by every anti-aircraft gun in the Ruhr valley - or so it seemed at the receiving end. Now D-Donald was coned and it was our turn to receive the exclusive attention of the wrathful German gunners.

I had been told to put the Lancaster's nose down, open the throttles and get out of the area quickly. Flying fast also presented a more difficult target for the gunners below. In a moment, we were nose-down at an angle of about 30 degrees, engines screaming, wings flapping, fuselage shaking and the airspeed indicator showing almost 400 miles per hour. We dropped about 5000 feet very quickly. Sometimes pilots could be lucky and this time the tactic worked as we extended the searchlights to the point where they could no longer hold on to us. Thankfully they gave up.

Back in darkness, we found that the intense glare had blinded us. We blinked our eyes, gathered our wits about us and made a run on Mulheim to drop our bomb load. We learned later that our starboard inner fuel tank had been holed by anti-aircraft fire, so we were lucky to have survived the experience. Not many did!

Next morning, we took off on a fighter affiliation exercise. The idea was for a Spitfire to make attacks on our Lancaster with his special camera guns operating and for us to reply with ours. This was practice for both of us, he in attack, we in defence.

All went well until an American Thunderbolt joined in and before long we were spectators as the two fighters, Spitfire and Thunderbolt, engaged each other. There really was no competition as the nippy Spitfire flew round and round its heavy opponent, outmanoeuvring it time and time again. Like the Lancaster, the Spitfire was a magnificent aircraft, both designed to do a job in which both were without peers.

In the briefing room that evening, we were told our 'target for tonight' . It was Wuppertal. The date was the 24th June, 1943.

CHAPTER 2

WUPPERTAL

Target briefing was scheduled for 1700 hours and the briefing room was almost full when we arrived about 5 minutes early. Behind the rostrum, the large, now familiar wall map of Europe was covered so as not to reveal too early, the target for that night.

Waiting to break the news to the assembling aircrew was the Commanding Officer, Wing Commander C. E. Martin, D.S.O., D.F.C. With him were the Meteorological Officer, the Flying Control Officer, the Intelligence Officer and other section commanders.

By 1700 hours there was a noisy buzz of anticipation from over one hundred edgy aircrew. Some were betting on where Bomber Command was likely to leave its calling cards that night. Others just sat and waited, restless, impatient to know. A few were boisterous, talkative, maybe to cover up deeper feelings. The doors were closed and secured by armed service police.

Then a hush as Wing Commander Martin rose to speak, "Gentlemen, the target for tonight is Wuppertal in the Ruhr."

A moan of mock disbelief filled the room, "Bloody hell, surely not Happy Valley again," whispered someone close by. The wall map of Europe was uncovered, already marked with pins, traced with coloured cord showing our rendezvous point, course to the Dutch coast, our approach to the target and the route back to Binbrook.

Wing Commander Martin continued, "Shortly, the various leaders will tell you of the conditions you'll encounter over enemy territory. For my part, let me say how very important this target is. Wuppertal is comprised of two centres, Elberfield and Barmen. This raid is centred on the Elberfield half. Bomber Command has already targeted Barmen on the 29th May, this year. That raid was most successful. I can't say too much but we know that there are factories in Wuppertal manufacturing parts for secret aircraft not yet in service in the Luftwaffe. At least now you know that it is of utmost importantance that these factories are destroyed." He went on, "These twin raids are the first on Wuppertal, tonight's operation, hopefully, completes the job. For the time being, anyway, that is. Your task is to ensure that this raid is as successful as the first so that we don't have to go back. I'll now call on the Intelligence officer to detail the route. A good strike and a safe return," he concluded, paraphrasing the Squadron's motto of "Strike and Return".

460's Intelligence Officer stood beside the wall map of Europe. "Take off is at 2230 hours, "A" flight first, then "B" flight." He detailed the coordinates of the rendezvous point over The Wash, time and height over the Dutch coast and discussed in depth the course into Wuppertal.

"Elberfield is to the west of Barmen so you've been routed in between Dusseldorf and Krefeld. These cities are heavily defended so straying to starboard or port makes you an easy target for their anti-aircraft and searchlight batteries. 460 Squadron is due over the target at 0035 hours, 20,000 feet, so there should be plenty of red target indicators, otherwise bomb on the greens, of course. Route home is south around Cologne and then west back to base. Further details for the navigators at their briefing later on."

The meteorological officer told us of the weather conditions we might encounter. "Moonlight and little cloud means ideal conditions for German fighters," he warned.

Next the Armaments Officer described our bomb load, "You'll carry 1 x 4000lb high capacity "cookie", 2 x 500lb general purpose, 1 x 500lb delay action, 6 cans 30lb explosive incendiary and 7 cans 4lb incendiary, just over 11,000lbs all up. I will discuss bomb sight settings later with the bomb-aimers." The Gunnery Officer again warned of the possibility of attacks by night fighters because of the clear weather conditions. "Rear and mid upper gunners stay behind in this room afterwards, for a further briefing," he ordered.

Finally we broke up into our various musterings, pilots to the flight offices, navigators to the navigation office and so on. After these individual briefings, we went to the mess and ate a nervous supper, hoping that our next meal would be the ritual return "breakfast" of real eggs and bacon. It was privilege reserved exclusively for aircrew on their return from Germany.

We had a free hour or so on our hands before we were due at D-Donald's dispersal and we went to our billets, supposedly to relax. No way!! Our minds were too full of what we had to do during the next few hours. Each went over and over his job as an aircrew team member, never contemplating the worst that could happen; just checking mentally all that we had been trained to do and told during the briefing. One slip by any one of us could endanger the whole crew.

Growing impatient and tired of ruminating, I got up, telling my crew to follow when they were ready. I collected my "deliverance", my parachute, from the store and caught an early vehicle to D-Donald's dispersal area, which was already buzzing with activity.

The armourers had already done their job. With bomb bay doors still hanging menacingly open, D-Donald displayed its cavernous 33 foot bomb bay, brim-full of high explosives and incendiaries. As I looked, I realised that the Lancaster was nothing more than a huge flying bomb bay. The massive 4000lb "cookie" dominated, surrounded by high explosive and delay action 500 pounders and cans of fiery incendiaries. Transported from the ammunition dump on long trolley trains, one load could blow the whole aerodrome to kingdom come. That any bomber could fit one complete train load into its bomb bay and then become airborne, seemed unbelievable. The mighty Lancaster took the lot with ease.

Standing underneath, I shuddered as I looked up at 11,000 lbs of death and destruction that would be multiplied by the 700 odd aircraft that would attack Wuppertal that night. The futility and stupidity of it all crossed my mind. Doubts? Perhaps, but then I thought of London and Coventry.

Small arms ammunition was still being loaded into the three gun turrets to feed eight Browning .303 inch machine guns. Bedford tankers were topping up wing tanks to 1500 gallons (maximum 2200 gallons) of high octane fuel. It was a scene that was being repeated for the 14 other 460 Squadron aircraft on that

THE GIGANTIC BOMB BAY OF A LANCASTER BOMBER.

*A 'COOKIE' BOMB BEING LOADED ONTO
A LANCASTER BOMBER.*

night's Battle Order and for hundreds of others throughout England, for that matter.

Riggers and mechanics had methodically checked the aircraft from wing tip to wing tip, from bomb aimer's bubble to rear turret.

Finally, after the tankers had backed away, D-Donald was ready for its four Rolls Royce Merlin engines to be run up and tested. This last inspection was done from the aircraft's cockpit by an expert, the ground staff flight sergeant engineer. He checked oil and coolant temperatures, OK. Oil pressure, OK. Bomb doors closed, flaps down and up, brakes operating, hydraulics OK. Navigation lights, OK. Instruments, OK. Magnetos.... Damn!! A problem. A drop in revolutions on No.4!!

Merlin engines have two magnetos and the serviceability test is to run the engine up to 1000 RPM then switch off each of the magnetos in turn. If there's an appreciable drop in revolutions on either one, then that 'maggie' is declared unserviceable. Our starboard outer had a defective magneto! I looked at my watch. "Hey Flight, you only have about forty minutes to fix it before take off," I yelled from the ground. "You'd better get a move on."

Then my crew arrived. "Get aboard and check your equipment. We have maggie trouble and the Flight Sergeant is doing a slow march," I said impatiently. With ten minutes to spare, the new maggie was installed.

The problem having been solved, I was brought back to earth. My pre-occupation with the magneto had pushed Wuppertal into the back of my mind.

CORPORAL JIM NUTTALL AND OUR DISPERSAL VAN DRIVER PEGGY - TAKEN JUST BEFORE THE WUPPERTAL RAID.

Soon we would again take off for the dreaded "Happy Valley". Anticipation, tension and a hint of suppressed fear began to mount. With a fatalistic shrug, I crawled over the main spar and into the cockpit.

I started all engines and checked each of the starboard outer's magnetos for revolution drop. They were OK now. Next, I ran all engines up with Col' Broadbent, flight engineer, checking pressures, temperatures, hydraulics and instruments. All were serviceable. Control movements were free.

On the intercom, I contacted Col', Clarrie, Norm, Denis, Frank and Rowdy. All of their intercoms were OK. I asked Col. to tell the Flight Sergeant to bring me the Form 700 upon which I confirmed that the aircraft was OK.

I signed it and quipped that they were, "Just in time with the maggie."

"What else, Skipper?" was the flight sergeant's return as he climbed back over the wing spar. I signalled 'chocks away'. Then with a touch on the throttles, D-Donald began to roll forward.

Dusk was falling and with propellers lazily ticking over we joined the queue of 14 aircraft waiting their turn to take off. It seems we had to queue for everything during wartime. The staccato crackle of 60 restless Merlin engines signalled 460 Squadron's resolve to "Strike and Return" that night.

At 2223 hours a green flare from the duty pilot and the first aircraft rolled forward, turned left, then accelerating, disappeared over a crest on Binbrook's peculiar runway, to appear again, as it struggled heavily laden into the air.

Directly in front of us was G-George, skippered by Flying Officer J. R. Henderson. This aircraft incredibly survived 100 operations, and was later flown to Australia to be installed as a permanent exhibit in the War Museum in Canberra.

One by one the Squadron became airborne, while we waited, with Col watching our engine temperatures like a hawk. Too high and we would have had to shut them down to cool them off. G-George took off and then it was our turn on the runway.

First a burst of throttles, then I turned left and lined up with the runway. I put down 10 degrees of flaps, pitch full fine, mixture rich, trim controls centre, then checked with Col'. "OK?" Brakes on; throttles to 1000 revolutions; a 'green' from the duty pilot's Aldis lamp and I released the brakes. D-Donald trundled forward, slowly at first, then accelerated. A slight swing to the left was corrected by 'leading' the left two throttles in advance of the right. As the slipstream increased, the control column was pushed forward to raise the tail. Quickly, 50 M.P.H. was reached; direction control established using rudders; throttles fully forward and I handed them over to Col who made sure they were fully home against the gate. He tightened the friction nut, locking them. Engines 3000 revolutions per minute (R.P.M.); boost +14 lb/sq.in.; speed 110 M.P.H. and I eased back on the control column.

D-Donald reluctantly heaved itself, 1500 gallons of fuel, 11,000lbs of bombs and seven human beings into the air. 130 M.P.H.; undercarriage up; 140 M.P.H.; flaps up; 160 M.P.H.; engines down to +9 lb/sq.in. boost, 2850 R.P.M. Colin checked oil and coolant temperatures. All were OK. I trimmed the control surfaces for climb as we reached 500 feet.

"What's the course to the rendezvous point, Clarrie?"

"150 degrees magnetic, skipper. E.T.A. (estimated time of arrival) at rendezvous point 2251hrs at 10,000 ft."

On course now, D-Donald dragged itself higher, engines roaring with the toil of it. Dusk became night as the sun finally disappeared over the western horizon.

"We're wowing a bit, Col." Engines out of synchronisation develop an annoying oscillating drone above the usual roar. It is caused by one motor rotating at a slightly different speed than the others. Col made the necessary adjustments to throttle and pitch lever settings and soon the irksome drone was gone.

"How long to the rendezvous point, Clarrie?" I glanced at the altimeter. "We're at 7800 feet now."

"About four minutes - but we're too early by about a minute and a half," he replied.

Without thinking, I made a 360 degree turn to port to lose time. I should have realised that there were dozens of heavy bombers in the vicinity, all streaming east. D-Donald, on the other hand, was now for a time flying west against this stream. How we did not collide with another bomber I will never know. I had been very stupid and we had been very lucky.

At least we were now on time, at 10,000 feet and at the rendezvous point. I told everyone to put on their oxygen masks. Unless you are acclimatised, breathing gets pretty difficult above 10,000 feet without extra oxygen, and we were about to climb much higher.

I asked Clarrie for a course to the Dutch coast. "120 degrees magnetic and climb on to 20,000 feet, skipper. Estimated Time of Arrival (ETA) Dutch coast 2355 hours," he answered.

We had been routed over Grevelingen (waterway) between Rotterdam and Antwerp, to avoid the anti-aircraft defences concentrated around these two cities. Nevertheless the Luftwaffe night fighter squadrons based in Holland would certainly be on the lookout for us, so Rowdy and Frank had to keep their eyes skinned. I checked with them over the intercom.

"We were all eyes long ago, skipper," Rowdy said.

At 15,000 feet the cold started to bite, even though it was summertime. Those of us in the main cabin were not in heated flying suits, as we would have been in winter. The effort involved in corkscrewing the aircraft to the target and back would soon warm me up. The gunners were OK, supposedly snug in their sometimes not-too-effective flying suits. On the other hand, the navigator and particularly the wireless operator, were soon to be sweltering because the heating duct from our port-inner engine entered the cabin near their seats. The bomb aimer and engineer probably felt a little chilly but they would soon be 'warmed' by the tensions of time and place. Even our mighty Lancasters had their design faults, it seemed.

Lancasters had an automatic pilot, nicknamed 'George', which was not used in action, as at no time were you flying in one direction and at a constant speed and height for more than a minute or two. I do not remember ever using George whilst flying Lancasters, except for a short time to become familiar with it.

"20,000 feet and the Dutch coast five minutes away," Clarrie reported and shortly after, below us was Holland's southern coast. The moon's reflection on the water outlined two large peninsulas jutting out into the sea, with Shouwen and Walcheren to the south, and to the north Voorne.

"Cruising revs', Col, +4 lb/sq.in. boost and try 1800 R.P.M." Straight and level, D-Donald held 160 mph of indicated air speed (I.A.S.).

"Course change, skipper," Clarrie reported. "104 degrees magnetic. Distance to Wuppertal 145 miles, E.T.A. 0035 hours. We'll be passing between Duisburg and Dusseldorf just before the target so it'll get pretty hot." I had Col' increase throttle settings a little to compensate for the loss of ground speed due to corkscrewing.

"Try 2000 R.P.M. as well," I suggested as I pumped away at the control column. Over to our left and at about the same height, I saw a bright flash of light that slowly faded and finally vanished.

"Probably a collision between two 'friendlies'." I shuddered. "Another 14 airmen gone." I said nothing to the crew.

Collisions between attacking aircraft accounted, we were told, for an increasing number of losses in Bomber Command. Aircraft were scheduled to arrive over the target in waves two minutes apart and at various heights. Even so, bombers were sometimes late in arriving or were at other than their allotted heights, maybe due to navigational or mechanical problems. Still, there were plenty of aircraft in your wave and at your height to bother about. So your life and the lives of thirteen others depended on the vigilance and competence of all. Quite a responsibility for 20 year-olds.

I saw another explosion, this time on the ground, far below. Most likely a bomber, attacked by a fighter, crashed, bombs and all. I hoped somebody parachuted before the aircraft hit the deck. Fat chance!!

We could see Wuppertal, ablaze, in front of us and still ten miles away. Dozens of searchlights speared skywards around the now-familiar box barrage of exploding anti-aircraft shells. Green and red target indicators confirmed the presence of our Pathfinder force. Heavy bombers were as thick as flies, thankfully all going in somewhat the same direction. Some above us, possibly early or late arrivals, were getting ready to drop their bombs on the target and on D-Donald as well. Others below us, silhouetted against the fires, were positioned to accept our load. The seemingly impregnable wall of fiery anti-aircraft bursts was closing fast. Probing searchlights seeking their prey, were much too close. Only a few Luftwaffe fighters, though. Too dangerous over the target for them, I guessed. Most attacked the bombers before the target or afterwards on the trip home. Only the bravest and the most dedicated member of a Nachtjagdgeschwader (Night hunter squadron) faced his own flak.

Possibly we were too close to Dusseldorf. Or maybe it was just that "Jerry" was everywhere that night. Suddenly, like Mulheim only two nights before, night was turned into day. We were again coned by searchlights. I repeated the same procedure as was successful then. Stop corkscrewing. Nose down. Throttles open. Go like hell. The faster you go the harder you are to hit. Get out of the area as quickly as possible.

*AN AIRCRAFT 'CONED' BY
SEARCHLIGHTS OVER 'HAPPY VALLEY'.*

Once more D-Donald flapped its wings, motors screamed and its fuselage shook violently. Clarrie reported our air speed as over 400 M.P.H. Heavy with bombs, we quickly dropped from 20,000 feet to 15,000 feet and were just about clear when I saw two bright yellow flashes, in quick succession, over the nose of the aircraft.

I heard the "clump, clump" of two exploding flak shells, then a noise like hail on a tin roof and I swore I smelt cordite.

We had received multiple direct hits from a German anti-aircraft battery.

"Bloody Hell, the starboard inner engine's on fire, skipper," yelled Col'.

I glanced to my right where tongues of red flames were already straddling the wing and number two fuel tank. It could explode at any moment. "Kill it fast. NOW!!" I ordered.

Col' immediately throttled the engine back and feathered its propeller. He quickly pressed the red fire extinguisher button for that engine. Thank Heaven the extinguisher did its job and the fire went out. The port inner engine had simply stopped.

"Feather it as well." Hell, what next? Quickly I opened the bomb bay doors. There was an ominous glow coming from the area where the cans of incendiaries were hanging.

"Jettison the bomb load FAST, Norm. I think the incendiaries have been hit and are alight." He did not have to be told twice and I felt the aircraft jump up as 11,000lbs of bombs fell away. There was no doubt we had jettisoned them just in time!! Suddenly we were free of the searchlights. Perhaps they could not hold us any longer or they knew they had clobbered us and went looking for other game.

"Anyone hit?" I checked the crew and recognised the voices of Norm, Col', Clarrie and Dennis. All unhurt.

"You OK Rowdy, Frank?" God, no reply!! Fearfully I sent Dennis back to check. They were OK. It was the intercom' to the gun turrets that was out.

We were down to 12,500 feet as we flew over the target and at that height we were as vulnerable as Wuppertal down below. We could have been hit by any one of thousands of bombs and incendiaries raining down on us from our own bomber force 7000 feet above.

"Skipper, the bomb bay doors are still open," Norm reported. There was no way of closing them on this aircraft with both inner engines stopped.

"And I can see the starboard undercarriage hanging halfway down," Col' said.

"The port under-cart too," said Clarrie looking over my shoulder.

"We can't retract them without hydraulics," said Col'.

Corkscrewing was out, as even when flying straight and level, we were losing height. The extra drag of the open bomb bay and the undercarriage was the problem. The two remaining outer engines were flat out. Boost +9lbs/sq.in., 2850 R.P.M. (1 hour limit). Desperately we tried other throttle and pitch settings but D-Donald continued to lose height so we jettisoned everything moveable, even some of our fuel. Later we released the carrier pigeon with a message but would it find its way back to England?

According to the Pilot's Notes, the Lancaster could hold height at 10,000 feet on two engines and I had done so as an exercise plenty of times at the Conversion Unit. Was there other damage affecting performance, I thought. The crew reported extensive fuselage damage, mostly holes and rips in the aluminium skin. Possibly the wings were holed as well.

Count your blessings! Someone had been looking after us and we were lucky:

* Two simultaneous direct hits by anti-aircraft shells.
* Both inner engines knocked out, one on fire.
* Considerable damage to the fuselage and possibly the wing surfaces.
* The bombs had not exploded.
* It seemed the incendiaries had burst into flames.
* We were still flying and under control.
* Nobody seemed to be seriously hurt, although we later found that Rowdy had a flak wound in his leg.
* With very little encouragement, the thin-skinned 'cookie' could have blown us to kingdom come and back, with the help of even the smallest piece of shrapnel.
* If we were attacked by a fighter, the gunners had no way of contacting me with evasion instructions - we were a sitting duck for even the Red Baron in his Fokker Triplane.

"Unfeather the port inner engine, Col'. Maybe it'll rotate fast enough to generate hydraulic pressure and raise the bomb bay doors and under-cart." No joy!! We lost height even faster.

"Feather the bloody thing again," I said. Clarrie gave me a course south, then west towards the coast. Still straight and level, we flew around Cologne and at 0125 hours we crossed over the German/Belgian border. Ever losing height, we were now down to 3500 feet and through the darkness, I could make out features on the ground below.Thankfully there were no fighters, as they were, most likely, taking care of the main stream above and in front of us.

Soon I would have to make a decision. Either I give the order to bail out straight away or hold on, hoping D-Donald would maintain height in the lower, heavier atmosphere. The trouble was we were approaching the point of no return. Soon we were going to be too low to take to our parachutes anyway. The third alternative was a forced landing at night. I quickly ruled this out as a quick way to oblivion for my six crewmen.

We were about 20 miles north-north-west of Liege, Belgium and still we dropped. At 2500 feet, Col' reported that the temperature of the starboard outer was off the clock and it could seize at any moment. "No oil pressure," he said.

That did it! Without hesitation, I ordered, "ABANDON AIRCRAFT!! ABANDON AIRCRAFT!!" However, with the intercom unserviceable, the gunners had no way of knowing that we were about to bail out. I told Dennis to go back fast and see if Rowdy and Frank had gone yet.

Meanwhile, Norm had jettisoned the escape hatch in the floor of the bomb-aimer's compartment, clipped on his chest parachute and without hesitation rolled out of the aircraft into the night. Next it was Col's turn. With a brave smile and a nervous wink he stepped down to the waiting hatchway, knelt on the edge and was gone.

Dennis clambered back over the main spar, "Rowdy and Frank have bailed out from the rear door, skipper," he said. "They'll be OK."

"Thanks Dennis. Off you go now. Be quick," I said, relieved.

Dennis followed Col out through the open hatch, leaving just Clarrie and me aboard. "Good luck, skipper," he said courageously as he handed me my parachute. "See you in Spain."

He checked twice to make sure my parachute was clipped on securely, then with a reassuring glance, disappeared into the night. D-Donald and I were alone. Just for a moment the ship's captain syndrome almost overcame me, as I felt sadness and shame because I was about to desert my mighty Lancaster.

Soon D-Donald would be no more. It was no consolation to me that many had already gone before and there would be many more to follow.

D-Donald and I were still losing height. Hurry, hurry, we were down to 2000 feet. I stood up to the right of the control column, keeping the aircraft straight and level with my left hand. Below the open hatchway waited and I hurried down and knelt at its edge.

Then, for a moment, I thought of the hundreds, no, thousands of aircrew who had attempted and were yet to attempt, to save their lives by abandoning their stricken aircraft, as I was about to do. For the vast majority, their desperate bid to stay alive would have been so different from my relatively orderly exit.

The stark terror of a spinning aircraft flashed through my mind, with all those on board gripped by irresistible centrifugal forces preventing escape. Maybe their aircraft was on fire, adding to their desperation. If wounded comrades were left behind, what future nightmares would memories of a 'last glance into terror stricken eyes' generate for he who survived? What turmoil invaded the minds of those who knew they were trapped and could do no more than await the inevitable!!

But I was lucky as all my brave crew were clear. All I had to do was roll forward and kindly D-Donald, still flying straight and level, would free me. The escape hatch on a Lancaster was 23 inches wide x 26 inches long and as I squatted there ready to jump, I found it difficult to imagine how anyone could get through such a small hole. Resigned to losing the top of my head as I rolled out or worse, getting stuck, I committed myself to fate and fell forward with my hand tightly gripping the rip cord.

For a moment the slipstream seemed determined to push me back into the aircraft. Suddenly I fell free - free to plummet into a fearful black void. As I tumbled over in the air, I saw the dark outline of D-Donald above me as it flew on alone. The slender fuselage, the broad rounded wings, the prominent four Merlins and the tailplane with its tall twin rudders, was a vision never to be forgotten. The trauma of the moment and that last glimpse of my Lancaster, are bound together in my memory forever.

A bone-shattering jerk and my parachute opened. Shaken and confused, I found myself hanging, perilously supported by a flimsy canopy of white silk above me. Recovering somewhat, I wished the W.A.A.F. airwoman who packed my parachute so carefully, a, happy and prosperous life. Relieved to have made it so far, the fact that I was suspended on silken threads 1,500 feet above the ground, was little comfort. Just as well it was dark.

I heard D-Donald's motors getting louder and louder as it went into its death dive. It seemed that it was turning back towards me to exact revenge because I had left it to its fate. Then an horrific explosion and a blinding flash close by and down to my left.

Vale D-Donald.

Small arms ammunition began to explode, chattering like machine-gun fire. Although the bullets were not going anywhere, I imagined that I was being fired upon in retribution. An occasional puff of wind and I swung gently back and forth. I could only just make out the ground, 1000 feet below me but luckily I was drifting away from the inferno that used to be my Lancaster.

I had heard terrible tales of parachutists landing in the fires of the cities they had just bombed, surviving only to face the wrath of the German populace. Others had come down in high winds and crashed into houses and fences. Many had been caught high in tree tops or buildings, hanging there, awaiting rescue by those who in anger, would just as rather leave them dangling, exhibited. I had also heard of an airman, having been blown out of his aircraft without a parachute, crashing down through the branches of a tall tree and landing in a snowdrift at its base; body badly broken - but alive.

460 SQUADRON

Year 1943		Aircraft		Pilot, or 1st Pilot	2nd Pilot, Pupil or Passenger	Duty (Including Results and Remarks)		
Month	Date	Type	No.					
						Totals Brought Forward		
June	22	Lancaster I	ED367	Self	and Crew	OPERATIONS MULHEIM		
						1 – 4000 LB HIGH CAPACITY		
						2 – 500 GENERAL PURPOSE		
						1 – 500 DELAY ACTION		
						6 – CANS 30LB EXPLOSIVE INC		
						6 – CANS INCENDIARY 4 LB		
						FLAK HEAVY CONED BY		
	24	III	F/O 220	P/O HENDERSON	SELF AND CREW	SEARCHLIGHTS.		
	24		E/O 730	SELF	P/O HENDERSON	FIGHTER AFFILIATION		
	24	I	W4322		AND CREW	FIGHTER AFFILIATION		
	24				AND CREW	A/C TEST		
	24					OPERATIONS. WUPPERTAL MISSING		

K.R.Grid. S/L O.C. A FLT.

W/CDR O.C. 460 SQDN.

FLYING LOG BOOK
OPERATIONS, WUPPERTAL, MISSING

Grand Total [Cols. (1) to (10)] Hrs. Mins.
Totals Carried Forward

AUTHOR'S LOG BOOK EXTRACT

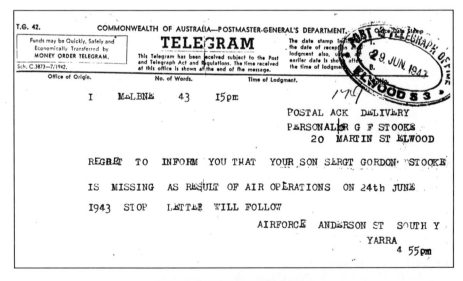

T.G. 42. COMMONWEALTH OF AUSTRALIA—POSTMASTER-GENERAL'S DEPARTMENT.

TELEGRAM

Funds may be Quickly, Safely and Economically Transferred by MONEY ORDER TELEGRAM.
Sch. C.3873—7/1942.

This Telegram has been received subject to the Post and Telegraph Act and Regulations. The time received at this office is shown at the end of the message.

The date stamp In the the date of reception a lodgment also, u earlier date is sho the time of lodgmen

29 JUN 1943
ELWOOD S 3

Office of Origin. No. of Words. Time of Lodgment.

I MELBNE 43 15pm

POSTAL ACK DELIVERY
PERSONAL MR G F STOOKE
20 MARTIN ST ELWOOD

REGRET TO INFORM YOU THAT YOUR SON SERGT GORDON STOOKE

IS MISSING AS RESULT OF AIR OPERATIONS ON 24th JUNE

1943 STOP LETTER WILL FOLLOW

AIRFORCE ANDERSON ST SOUTH Y
YARRA
4 55pm

OFFICIAL 'MISSING' TELEGRAM

None of this was for me; it seemed I was to be one of the lucky ones. As I drifted down towards the open fields far below, I rejoiced in my deliverance, although with considerable trepidation.

Suddenly and threateningly Belgium rushed up towards me. A parachute landing was equivalent to jumping off a 12 foot wall, but at height, the rate of descent was not noticeable. Near the ground it was as if my parachute had collapsed. I hit hard and sprained both ankles. Maybe we should have been better trained as parachutists but I guess aircrew were supposed to fly aeroplanes, not jump out of them.

I had plunged into a field near an amazed cow, that reared back in fright, wondering, no doubt, where the devil I had come from.

Oh well, better Belgium with sprained ankles than Uranus*.

Or worse, hearing the bark of Cerberus*.

*URANUS - Heaven in Greek mythology
*CERBERUS - Many headed watchdog of Hades, the realm of the dead.

CHAPTER 3

MERCI LA BELGIQUE

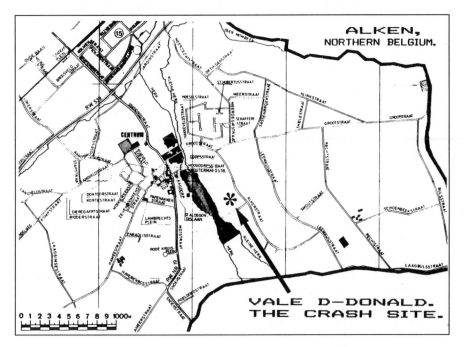

THE CRASH SITE IN ALKEN - NORTHERN BELGIUM.
VALE D-DONALD

I guessed that it would not be long before the whole area was alive with searching Jerry troops and my best bet was to get as far away from the crash site as possible - fast.

According to the book, I was supposed to bury my parachute, my "Mae West", and my flying helmet. I reckoned it would take too long, so I gathered everything up into a bundle and hid it under a hedgerow. Most likely it would be found later but by then I would be long gone and far away.

There was about three hours of darkness left so, even with my sprained ankles, I should be able to travel at least ten miles before dawn.

The glow of D-Donald's death pyre was to the north of me. That was great, since the classic escape route out of Europe was south through France and then, Spain.

I looked at my watch and it had stopped at 0146 hours. It must have been damaged as I squeezed through the escape hatch or when I landed.

Climbing through a hedge, I found a southbound two-wheeled furrowed track on the other side.

I hobbled on painfully, often stumbling in the dark on the rutted surface. I had to stop and rest more often than I liked as the pain in my ankles worsened. It seemed that something must have been broken and ten miles travel before dawn was out of the question.

From time to time, I could hear the drone of heavy aircraft engines overhead. It was too late for them to have been R.A.F. aircraft so they must have been Luftwaffe Nachtjagers returning from their deadly game of cat and mouse with Bomber Command.

By about three o'clock I was too tired to go on. The pain was unbearable so I rested for about half an hour. Then, worried that I might still be too close to the crash site, I gritted my teeth, took a deep breath and stumbled painfully on.

The track had become a good-sized road, still heading south and I passed through a number of small villages but saw no one. It was just as well, because I was still in full R.A.A.F. battle dress with all insignia showing - a little unusual in 1943, on a lonely road in German-occupied Belgium at 4 o'clock in the morning.

Twice I heard light aircraft low overhead, maybe spotting for survivors from D-Donald's crash. I wondered how my crew were getting along and whether any of them had been captured yet. Later I found out that all had survived, but unknown to me, Rowdy Nowlan, Rear Gunner, had copped a load of flak in his leg over Wuppertal. After a most painful landing, he found his way to the same German hospital as the mid-upper gunner, Frank Shaw, who had unfortunately broken his leg on landing.

Just before dawn I saw a farmhouse, more remote than others and with a small shed, about twenty yards from the house. Not the best of hiding places but it would have to do. I guessed that I was at least eight painful miles from where I had 'dropped in' on Belgium, so it was unlikely that German troops would be searching so far away.

As quietly as I could, I opened the door of the shed and crept in. It was as black as pitch inside but I gingerly lay down on the dirt floor and dozed off into a fitful sleep.

Suddenly I was wide awake. I was no longer alone - a frail old lady was pottering about outside, doing her daily chores.

I guessed it to be late mid-morning and through cracks and missing planks in my shed, I could clearly see her house. A road led down to a small village, 200 yards away.

The old lady swept her path, went inside for a time then came out again to laboriously pump water from her well. Back inside her house again, I supposed she was preparing a midday meal as I did not see her for about two hours.

Meanwhile I went through my pockets and of all things, found my Tonette. This was a small musical instrument like an Ocarina, bought in Australia before the war - not that I could play it very well but I enjoyed trying. That shed in northern Belgium was certainly not the place to practice. Next I examined my R.A.F. issue escape kit which included a silk escape map, water purifying tablets, chocolate, French francs and a compass. Hungrily I ate one square of the chocolate.

It seemed that my hiding place was a woodshed and outside, farm people walked past with some pushing carts along the roadway. Children played happily, never coming near the house or my woodshed. My old lady was certainly a loner. Perhaps her menfolk had been taken to labour camps in Germany as many other Belgians had.

At about 3 o'clock in the afternoon, the old lady again came out of her house and headed straight for the woodshed. I feared that it was time for her to light her fire and that she needed firewood. It had to come sometime. I was about to be discovered but strangely I felt more concern about the shock the old lady would get when she discovered me, than about being found. She opened the door, saw me and recoiled violently. Hurriedly I said in my schoolboy French, "N'ayez pas peur, n'ayez pas peur. Je suis Anglais." (Don't be afraid, don't be afraid. I am English.") There was no point in saying that I was Australian.

She backed away a few steps, hesitated and closed the woodshed door, and did not say a word. I suspected she was Flemish and did not understand me. She was probably too frightened to speak, anyway. She went back inside her house.

What should I do? I could not leave and wander around the Belgian countryside at 4 o'clock in the afternoon in an R.A.A.F. uniform. If I stayed where I was, my old lady may have gone for help of the wrong kind - the wrong kind for me. But she had not. She returned, bringing an apple and a glass of milk - a motherly act that convinced me that my best bet was to put myself in her hands. She motioned me to stay where I was and shortly after I saw her hobble down to the village.

I realised then how vulnerable I was. For the first time in my life I had lost freedom of movement and fluency. I had lost control of my destiny. I was trapped. Outside my shed was danger and menace - inside confinement and fearful anticipation. No longer the glamorous airman strutting around London, I was instead a nervous 20-year old boy contemplating a most uncertain future.

An hour later my old lady came back, not with the German Geheimefeldpolizei (Secret Police) that I had been half expecting, but with two male farm people.

"Bonjour, Monsieur," [Good-day, Sir] I said in friendly fashion,

"Bonjour, Anglais," [Good-day, Englishman] one replied.

I felt it was about time for me to establish my nationality.

"Monsieur, je suis Australien," [Sir, I am Australian] I said proudly.

I think he said 'so what' in French or Flemish, but I was not sure.

I told them my name, rank and number but either they did not understand me or were not interested. I showed them my dog tags and the contents of my escape kit. Only the silk map impressed them. Conversation was pretty difficult as they were Flemish farm people and only spoke French "un petit peu" [a little bit]. Understanding came only after much gesticulation and pantomime. The questions they asked showed that they were suspicious of me and were trying to satisfy themselves that I was a genuine "Anglais". A couple of times I thought they spoke German but I had not the vaguest idea what they said and must have shown it. Finally they accepted me.

They had brought an old coat and a peaked cap to cover my uniform. I put the coat on, donned the cap and tried to look as much like a Flemish farmer as I could. They said I should follow them but about 50 metres behind. They understood that my ankles were sore, and so I might have to walk slowly.

As we left, I thanked my frail old lady as best I could, still conscious of the frightful shock I must have given her when she discovered me in her woodshed.

Dusk was falling as I nervously followed my guides along the road and through the village. It was hard to believe that only 24 hours before, also at dusk, I had been at the controls of D-Donald, following other 460 Squadron Lancasters along the taxi path towards Binbrook's runway and then Wuppertal.

I reflected on the reason why I had been told to stay some distance behind. I realised the frightful risk that people in German-occupied Europe took when they helped the enemies of the Third Reich. Even though their country was occupied, these unhappy people were treated as traitors if they opposed their new masters. Any excuse to send men and women to labour camps in Germany was good enough. And this was not restricted to the individual. Families were harassed because of the patriotic actions of one of their kin. A firing squad was an often-used alternative. All over occupied Europe, men and women who helped evaders were truly the bravest of the brave.

My guides stopped in front of a house in the next village, spoke to a woman and then gestured for me to go inside. Only the woman followed me. She was middle-aged and it was a relief to find she spoke French. Unfortunately I could only understand a little of what she said. How I wish I had taken more notice of my French teacher, "Mousy" McKean, at school.

"Avez-vous de l'argent?" [Have you any money?] she asked. It seemed that money was important everywhere, no less so in occupied Europe.

"Oui," I replied, proud of my understanding. "Francs Francais."

Spurred on by my comprehension, she rattled on so quickly that I only caught a word or two.

"Lentement" [Slowly], I begged.

The upshot was that she exchanged my French francs for Belgian francs and gave me another apple and a glass of milk.

It was dark when her husband and another man arrived. They told me that they would lead me to the railway station at Sint Truiden (St Trond) where someone was waiting to give me further instructions.

This was the first time I had been able to pinpoint myself geographically. In the woodshed I had tried to locate my position using my silk map. The problem was that I did not know exactly where my aircraft had come down. Later I found out that it was Alken, 7 miles north-east of Sint Truiden/St Trond.

As I staggered south the previous night, I must have gone close by Sint Truiden. Just south of the town was one of the Luftwaffe's biggest nightfighter aerodromes, II./Nachtjagergruppe 1 (2nd Squadron of Night Fighter Wing No. 1). This was one of the main links in the chain of defences protecting the Ruhr Valley.

I wondered what sort of welcome I might have received last night had I stumbled onto II.NJG 1. I thought of the chivalry of the First World War, when captured enemy pilots were given the freedom of the officers' mess and

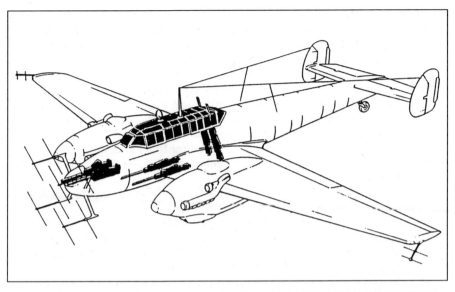

*MAJOR HEINZ-WOLFGANG SCHNAUFER'S MESSERSCHMITT BF 110 G4/U1 EQUIPPED
WITH "SCHRAGE MUSIC" - TWO 20 MM CANNONS POINTED UPWARD*

entertained in a manner befitting a fellow airman. The next day would have been a bit of a letdown though – a sore head and a rough ride to a prison camp.

Later, I found out that St Trond II./NJG 1 was under the command of Hauptmann Helmut Lent, who destroyed no less than 100 British bombers before his death in October 1944.

Another pilot, Heinz-Wolfgang Schnaufer, rivalled and eventually surpassed Lent by shooting down 125 R.A.F. heavy bombers to become the dominant ace of the Nachtjagerband,. Oberleutnant Schnaufer, later Major, had joined Lent at St Trond in the spring of 1942.

The Gruppe operated planes called

*SCHNAUFER'S MACHINE-GUN
ARRANGEMENT - AMMUNITION DRUMS
COULD BE REPLACED IN-FLIGHT*

Messerschmitt Bf110 G4/U1s designed solely as night fighters. Schnaufer attributed much of his success to his crew, Radio Operator Fritz Rumpelhardt and Gunner Wilhelm Gansler. His courage and skill was demonstrated by his practice of closing to within 50 yards before firing.

He also shot down many bombers using the "Schrage Musik (Slanting Music)" arrangement of two 20mm cannons angled upwards. These were aimed at the belly of unsuspecting British aircraft. Care was necessary to ensure that only bombers that had dropped their load of bombs were attacked in this way, otherwise self-destruction would be the result of the bomb load exploding.

On the 25th May 1944, Schnaufer accounted for five Lancasters. This was not his most successful bag for, on the 22nd February 1945, he destroyed nine four-engined bombers in one night.

Nicknamed "The Night Ghost of St Trond", it is ironic to record that he was killed in a freak motor accident in France in 1950.

No doubt an avenging R.A.F. pilot drove the other car!!

It was dark and with two other men leading the way, after half an hour we came to the outskirts of a town. There was a railway station with its signal box and the name on the side was Sint Truiden/St Trond.

As I climbed the stairs on the outside of St.Trond's signal box, I saw that the railway platform was empty. No German soldiers. By then I had been in Belgium for 24 hours and not yet seen one. Not that I was exactly heartbroken. Just curious to see what the 'Ogre' looked like.

A roaring fire in a huge fireplace lit up the inside of the signal box, with its two rows of levers, operating points and signals, running down the centre of the room. As I entered, the signalman shook my hand warmly. He obviously knew of my coming. It was only then that I noticed my guides had gone - their link in the chain was complete.

The signalman was Walloon, a French-speaking Belgian, who also spoke a little English. He knew who I was and explained that in an hour, I was to catch a train to Landen, about seven miles to the south-west, a short trip of about twenty minutes or so. There I was to change trains for Gembloux, another 18 miles south-west. This train would leave Landen at approximately 0200 hours and the journey to Gembloux would take about an hour or so. Not the fastest train in Europe, it seemed.

In both trains, a conductor would collect the fare. I was to hand him a piece of paper on which the names Landen and Gembloux were written. I must act deaf and dumb and a little silly.

Considering the situation I was in, I did not think the latter would be too difficult.

By then people were waiting on the station below and in the distance I heard a train whistle. It was 2345 hours. The signalman told me to go to the platform and board the rear carriage of the train. This was for civilians, the front end being reserved for German soldiers. It seems that I was about to confront the enemy.

The train trundled into the station and I saw that he was right. The first two carriages were full of unfamiliar green uniforms. Just like soldiers everywhere, some were singing and generally making a racket. Others were sitting quietly contemplating or trying to sleep. Such was the way of all soldiers in transit. Was the 'Ogre' normal, human, after all?

I boarded at the back of the train, chose a compartment and sat between two very large men. One immediately attempted to engage me in conversation but I pointed to my ears and shook my head. He seemed to accept my disability, transferring his attention to the man on the other side of me.

A whistle sounded, the train jerked into motion and we were off. Soon the conductor came and I went through my deaf and dumb act once more, handed him the slip of paper with Landen written on it, along with a one-franc note. He gave me back my change (50 centimes I think) and a ticket.

Squashed between two large, chatting Belgians, I was off to Landen, Belgium, escorted by fifty or so German troops up front. As expected, the journey took about half an hour. Upon arrival, I struggled out from between the two large, talkative Belgians and stepped down on to the platform.

Landen was a small town on the main railway line between Liege and Brussels and a terminal for a number of other converging secondary lines. That night the station was crowded with people from St. Trond and others waiting for the main-line train.

Large groups of German troops stood around, maybe on their way to Brussels with a leave pass. There were far too many German troops for me. As well as the 50 odd I had disembarked with, Jerry was everywhere. I felt as though every one of them was after me.

A little panicky, I tried to find a notice pointing me to the Gembloux platform but there was not a sign, anywhere. Even if I had I found the right platform, I would have had to wait about an hour and a half for the Gembloux train.

Suddenly I felt vulnerable and a little afraid. I decided that my best bet was to get away from the railway station, then come back just before 2am or maybe the next day. Hopefully it might be less crowded then. I could be wrong though - the adage 'lost in a crowd' might make better sense.

I left the station and walked about a quarter of a mile down a road away from the town, into a wheat field and lay down, well concealed.

Suddenly all that had happened to me over the last twenty-four hours became real, profound. Pent-up fears and premonitions rushed to the surface resulting in an overwhelming feeling of utter dejection. I was desperately lonely - half a world from home - a young man abandoned, cold and unsheltered. Shivering, I cried myself into a fitful sleep.

I awoke at dawn and carefully looked over the top of the wheat towards the road. Nobody was about so I did a 'daily dozen' or two to warm up my many frozen parts.

A few people were making for the station and reasoning that I might as well be hung for a sheep as a lamb, I confidently joined them from a path that ran alongside the wheat field. Joining these commuters was more hazardous than I at first thought. Most walked the same road, met the same fellow-travellers and caught the same train, at the same time each morning. They may never have passed the time of day but at least they knew each other by sight. When a complete stranger joined their ranks from a path originating in a wheat field, questioning minds may well have wondered.

There needed to be only one, advantage-seeking "nark" in a hundred and the German police would be told, papers would be asked for and high hopes of escape would be shattered. For me the war would be most unpleasantly over.

However, unaccosted, I reached the Landen railway station.

"I must have been blind last night," I thought. Printed on a station identification sign was the word Gembloux!! How I missed it the previous night, I would never know. The sign also showed departure as 7am and the station clock showed the time to be already 6.45am.

Soon the train arrived and I boarded the last carriage. Three other people were in the compartment but they took no notice of me - too early in the morning for scintillating conversation, I supposed.

I showed the conductor the piece of paper with Gembloux written on it. He also accepted my deaf and dumb act, took my five franc note and gave me back my change.

The train stopped twice but nobody joined us. During the tedious, one-and-a-quarter hour journey I had a look at the country on both sides of the railway line. The region was mostly flat and almost entirely given over to wheat and barley fields, with a few small dairy herds here and there. We passed by many small villages, characteristically arranged with cottages clustered around the village church.

We arrived at Gembloux at 8.15am according to the station clock. This town was on the main railway line between Namur and Brussels. I left the railway station along with an assortment of farm workers, town folk and a few German soldiers. It would have been helpful if the signalman at St. Trond had told me what I was to do after I reached Gembloux. This minor oversight forced me to prepare a fresh plan of action but first I had to get out of town.

Using the sun and the time of day to orientate me, I headed south-west through Gembloux and out into the countryside. Only then was it safe to examine my escape map. These maps were extraordinary; cleverly multicolour-printed on lightweight silk, the detail and clarity were superb. Because they could be crammed into a small space they were easy to conceal. They could be tied around the waist under clothing or even used as a scarf.

The only Belgian town familiar to me, other than Brussels, was Mons. I had read of the bloody battles fought there during World War One. My silk map showed that Mons was not too far from the French border. So Mons became "Checkpoint 1".

I reasoned that if I acted furtively I would travel slower and would be more conspicuous. So as bold as brass and with no attempt at concealment, I tramped on through villages and past wheat fields for maybe two hours.

Tramping degenerated into hobbling as my ankles became very painful and I had to rest for a while - but where?

Then I heard what sounded like a train but instead it was an electric tram. The sight of it almost made a Melbourne man feel homesick. It stopped invitingly and I did what seemed to be expected of me and obediently climbed aboard.

Anyway, this was a chance to rest my tormented ankles.

My deaf and dumb act was again accepted by the conductor as was my five-franc note. I held two fingers up to represent two francs and he gave me a ticket and three francs change. I hoped that two francs was enough to get me to Mons, providing this tram was going to Mons, of course.

The tram was almost empty when I joined it. Half an hour later there were about a dozen passengers on board including two German soldiers - one an officer. They would not be too much of a problem as long as they stayed where they were; at the other end of the tram.

However, when it stopped again, another German soldier got on and sat down beside me.

This was a bit too much. So far I had been able to keep the "Bete Noir" at arm's length. But here I was elbowing him as the tram rocked and swayed. Although I had on a civilian coat and hat, my Australian air force blue trousers with military slab pockets and cuff ties were there for all to see. Also I was smoking my second last English "Players" cigarette which had a completely different aroma to continental brands.

I literally held my breath until the next stop. As I got off, the Jerry looked at me oddly and made as if to get off as well but the tram jerked into motion and he changed his mind.

Was I saved by the quick action of the driver? Did he know who I was? I would have liked to believe he did.

Just in case the Jerry soldier came looking for me or sent the German Police to do the job, I walked about a hundred yards along a street away from the tram line and waited. I could clearly see the place where I had left the tram. After half an hour nothing had happened, so I guessed that my German co-traveller had not noticed my Air Force trousers nor the aroma of the Players cigarette.

The rest on the tram had eased my ankles a little so I set off towards the south-west and what I hoped was the open country. Soon though, the area became urban again. Before long, one town almost joined another with people everywhere, going about their business.

Occasionally The Master Race in a staff car went by at high speed, showing scant consideration for man or beast.

I could not refer to my silk map here, without attracting attention. However, from previous checking, I guessed that I must be near but north of, the city of Charleroi. Soon I found myself in a busy town square with a tram terminal nearby. To reach "Checkpoint 1", I needed to know which tram, if any, went to Mons. Three trams were waiting to leave.

With much trepidation I approached a man in civilian clothes standing on the footpath.

"Bonjour Monsieur," I said brightly, "pouvez-vous me dire quel tramway je dois prendre pour Mons?" [Good day, Sir, could you tell me which tram I should take for Mons?]

"Alors vous etes Flamand," he said in friendly fashion, spotting my heavy accent. [So you are Flemish.] He then jabbered away gutturally, pointing and gesticulating at the trams.

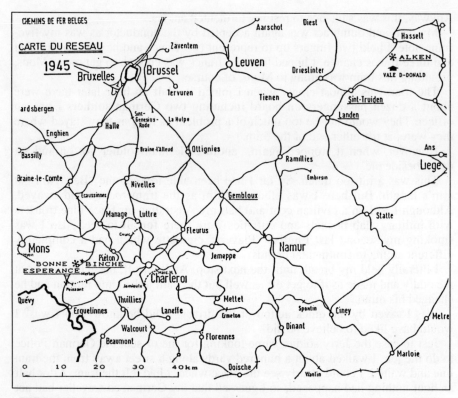

THE ROUTE FROM ALKEN TO BONNE ESPERANCE THAT THE AUTHOR TRAVELLED BY TRAIN, TRAM AND FOOT IN TWO DAYS.

Not understanding a word, taken completely by surprise, confused and not knowing that Dutch and Flemish were the same, I stupidly blurted out, "No I'm Dutch, but I haven't been there for a long time." The trouble was, I spoke in English! His face changed to a shocked ashen grey.

It was his turn to speak English, "That one over there. The green one," he whispered nervously, pointing towards the terminal. I had never seen anyone disappear as quickly as he did. He was off as if every Geheimefeldpolizei, Feldgendarmerie and Schutzstaffel in Belgium had heard our conversation and was after him. I would have bet on him being a patriotic Belgian, albeit dead scared. Nevertheless I decided it might be safer to miss this green tram but after noting which way it went.

I hobbled on for about two hours as the towns thinned out to villages and became countryside again. I felt very sore, hungry, utterly lonely and most concerned about where I was to spend that night. I reached the outskirts of another town, and a pretty big one judging by the number of church spires and clock towers on the horizon. There was no refuge here, so it was better to get back into the country again.

I turned due south, down a side road and soon there were wheat fields on either side. About half an hour later I came upon a farmer leading a horse and cart. I needed help as I did not want to face another freezing night in the wheat fields.

"Connaissez-vous quelqu'un qui parle Anglais, Monsieur?" I asked, fearing that this might well be the end of my bid for freedom. [Do you know someone who speaks English, Sir?]

"Oui Monsieur," he said without hesitation, "suivez-moi." [Yes Sir, follow me.] Five minutes later I saw a large clock-tower/belfry above the treetops.

"Abbaye de Bonne Esperance," the farmer informed me. [Abbey of Good Hope.] The way I was feeling, the Abbey was well named.

CHAPTER 4

ABBAYE DE BONNE ESPERANCE

The Abbaye was huge and dominated by a large two-storey building featuring a high clock tower. A steep snow-shedding attic roof added to its elevation and impressiveness. These and other similar buildings were surrounded by a high stone wall.

The farmer indicated that I should follow this wall around until I came to an entrance. "Anglaise" [English], he pointed over the wall and into the Abbaye.

"Merci Monsieur. Toujours la Belgique." [Thanks Sir] I said in appreciation [Belgium forever].

He went off towards a village close by which I later found out to be Vellereille les Brayeux.

Dusk was falling as I followed the wall, searching for an opening. Doubts swamped my mind as the fear and loneliness of the night before returned. Maybe it was all a hoax and there was nobody in the Abbaye who spoke English. Maybe my guide was even now heading for the German police to claim the resultant reward, following my capture.

I entered what I thought was the Abbaye, through a large open gate. Twenty feet inside, there was another opening under a long two-storey high gabled building. The half-cobbled and half-grassed courtyard measuring at least 75 yards long by 50 wide, was surrounded by similar two-storey buildings.

THE POST-WAR ABBAYE WITH THE FARM
AT THE BOTTOM CENTRE RIGHT.

There was much activity; men attending to and stabling heavy draught horses; others pitching hay into a big barn at the left end of the courtyard. At the right end was the farmhouse, with plenty of activity there, too. As I approached the door, I saw through a window, about a dozen people sitting at a large table eating.

Just about to knock, I hesitated as there were too many people around and I could not trust everyone. Better to try somewhere else, I thought as I backed away. Then a lady opened the kitchen door, "Puis-je vous aider, monsieur?" [Can I help you Sir] she asked.

"Oui Madame," [Yes Madame] "Y a-t-il quelqu-un ici qui parle Anglais?" [Is there someone here who speaks English] I said quietly. Quickly she took me aside. "Yes, I speak English," she said quizzically, suspiciously. Madame Alice Smeyers-Jurion was about forty years old. In an instant my fears of a few moments ago were gone. Do not ask me why but somehow I knew that for the moment anyway, I was safe.

She appeared not to return my confidence though. With my borrowed peak cap pulled down over my unshaven face and my ill-fitting coat and Air Force blue trousers covered in mud, I must have been a strange sight. Her English was perfect with a slight Irish accent. It appeared that she and her husband with their family, had spent a great deal of time in Ireland and still had friends there.

By this time I was almost crying and explained who I was, "I am a British airman shot down two nights ago and I need help," I told her. It was wonderful to speak and be understood. I started to show her my tunic under my old coat but she stopped me, "Too many farm people around," she said. As unobtrusively as possible she led me through the spacious kitchen where a meal was being served and into a small bedroom to the left.

"Are you hungry?" she asked.

My hearty "yes" was rewarded with a plate of thick soup. Even though it was almost hot enough to raise blisters, it disappeared in a flash.

"This is a large private farm serving the Abbaye Bonne Esperance and the surrounding area," she explained. "Many people work here during summertime so we have to be careful. It's not that they would report your presence to the Germans but they talk amongst themselves. A careless word here or there and we would be in deep trouble. I have a family to think of, you know. Oh, I notice you are limping badly, so rest and hot compresses for you.

Madame Smeyers-Jurion was right about having to consider her kinfolk as many families had been sent to German labour camps for a lot less. Shamefully, many had ended up in front of a firing squad.

She left me alone in the bedroom for about half an hour as she needed to talk things over with the family. I would have been less of a problem to them if I had arrived in winter, when only a few itinerant farm hands would be about. During summer harvest, with dozens of additional workers employed, hiding a British airman was a little hazardous. To make matters worse, I had come late in the day at the time when the men were in from the fields to eat and bed down.

When Madame Smeyers-Jurion returned, she said that I could stay for the night. Tomorrow other decisions would have to be made, because the dangers

THE SMEYERS BROTHERS JACKY, PAOLO, FRANZ AND JOHN.
PHOTOGRAPHED IN BELGIUM IN 1945.

were very real. She explained that they were leaving themselves wide open to tragic consequences if I was found by the German police.

"Wait in this room," she said, "I will send one of my sons in to talk with you. He will bring you more to eat." Soon a young man about my age, came in with bread and cheese.

"My name is Paolo Smeyers," he said, in good English with the same slight Irish accent. "Hope you like cheese." The way I wolfed it down left him in no doubt.

"First we will have to get rid of your uniform." I was not too keen on that idea because if I was captured, I was safer in uniform than civvies. Spies and saboteurs wore civvies and spies and saboteurs were shot! He sensed my reaction, "No hurry," he said quickly, "I'll introduce you to my family first."

It was now dark outside and the farmhands had gone to their sleeping quarters in the farm or to the village. We went into the kitchen. There was a cooking area through a door to the right and a large fire place to the left. Cupboards ran along the other side with a heavy table and chairs in the centre. At the back of the room was a door.

Paolo introduced his brothers, Jacky, Franz and John, who all showed keen interest in the Royal Air Force and flying. They asked many questions about my aircraft, life in England, etc. I felt a little ashamed at being guarded about what I said but that is how it was in 1943.

"We have a little sister too," said Jacky. "Her name is Blanche. She is asleep now." The other family members, Uncle Maurice Rochez and Aunt Aline Rochez-Jurion had a son named Leon, only two years old. Neither could speak English so unfortunately conversation with them was restricted.

Paolo explained that the family were not sure how grandfather Ernist Jurion would take the presence of an invader from the sky or whether he would go along with the risk the family were taking so they decided to try and keep my existence from him. "He's in bed now and tomorrow there'll be a lot of people around so he probably won't notice you, so long as you are wearing civvies," Paolo said hopefully.

Through the door at the back of the kitchen, he showed me a grassed area. Pointing to a vine-covered construction of an appropriate size in the corner, he said, "that's the toilet."

The following morning, after a fine farm breakfast and hot poultices applied to my ankles, Paolo came into my room with some old clothes.

"Try these on," he said. They fitted - a little loose here and a little tight there, but they would pass. I did not feel too happy to see my uniform go, but I made sure I kept my dog-tags. At least they would identify me as an airman should I be captured. I kept my silk map, compass, unserviceable watch, tonette and what was left of my escape kit.

Thoughts of London and strutting around Piccadilly Circus were now far, far away. For the time being, the glamorous, high-flying Lancaster pilot had become a simple Belgian farmhand.

As most of the men were out in the fields, I went into the courtyard for my morning ablutions. Two hefty pulls on the handle of a six foot-high water pump and I was showered with a cascade of pure, chilly water. Then, refreshed and fed, I felt like a new man, ready for whatever the day may have in store for me.

I spent the morning talking with Jacky in my room as there was less chance of attracting attention there. More importantly, I was away from Grandfather Jurion. I supposed that Paolo and the other Smeyers boys had gone about the business of the farm. Not so Paolo as I was soon to find out.

Jacky told me about the Abbaye de Bonne Esperance, its origin and its activities. The order was founded in 1127 but it wasn't until between 1734 and 1766 that the present massive complex was built. As well as a seminary, it became a college of secondary education. The attached farm controlled the land for kilometres around the Abbaye and until recently it had been run by the monks. Jacky smiled, "Happily it is now in the competent hands of the Jurion family."

During harvest time, the farm employed up to 40 workers. Even in winter, 12 or so were needed to look after the big draught horses. These people came from the surrounding villages such as nearby Vellereille les Brayeux. "Workers are hard to find these days," he explained. "It's whispered that at least 200,000 young Belgians have been forced to work in Germany."

Thirty-two mares and four stallions ensured the preservation of the breed and provided the horse-power to haul the carts that carried in the wheat, barley, beet and lucerne.

At the far end of the courtyard was a barn reputed to be the largest in

Belgium. It was about 150 feet long x 75 feet wide x 45 feet high. Its huge beams came from large oak trees that used to be in abundance in the area - a truly impressive building.

About midday Paolo returned. "We have made arrangements for you to stay with my close friend Yannick Bruynoghe in Arbre. It will be much safer for you there but the problem is that Arbre is about 80 kilometres from here."

I asked how he was able to get in touch with his friend so far away and tell him of me.

"By telephone," he replied and then smiled. "We have learnt how to talk freely over the 'phone yet completely confuse eavesdroppers. Can you ride a bicycle?" he added.

"Sure I can," I replied, "can't everyone? Anyway I had one on the Squadron." And then ruefully, "Some kleptomaniac has purloined it by now, I'll bet."

"Right, then you can have mine but we'll need to take all identification off it. You could easily be caught by the Germans on the way. Neither you nor the bike must ever be traced back to Bonne Esperance." All flippancy had disappeared - Paolo was deadly serious, "The family has decided that you must leave Bonne Esperance early tomorrow morning. It is too dangerous for all of us, you included, to hide at the farm any longer. We must plan carefully and choose the safest possible route between here and Arbre. There'll be less chance of running into German patrols if you travel on minor roads and pass through small villages."

A two by ten inch strip between Bonne Esperance and Arbre was cut from a

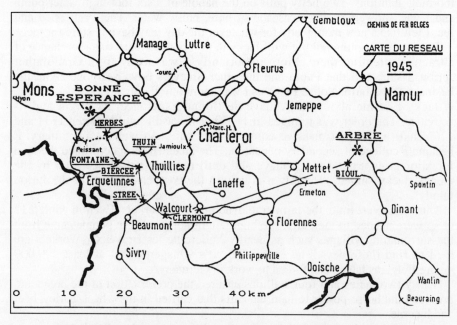

THE AUTHOR'S BICYCLE ROUTE FROM BONNE ESPERANCE TO ARBRE

road map. Being more detailed, we decided it would be better to use this rather than my silk map.

"As you cycle towards Arbre, you can tear off and throw away the part you've already travelled," Jacky pointed out. "That way the farm is secure should you be caught."

"We won't show any detail of the approaches to Arbre," Paolo added, "you will have to memorise that bit. As Jacky said, Bonne Esperance will be safe and so will my friend Yannick. You understand why we have to be careful, don't you? Now let's see. Go east along the road outside the Abbaye and you'll come to a main road. Turn south but look out for German patrols. Turn left at Merbes St. Marie, then right to Fontaine Valmont."

As he talked, I followed the route he had planned on the strip map. Except for the main road south out of Binche, all others were secondary. Obviously by being so careful, the chance of encountering German police or S.S. patrols would be minimal. "Left to Biercee then right to Stree and Clermont." Paolo described how I should go all the way to Arbre. "This part you must memorise. You are going to the Chateau de Marteau-Longe, the home of a student friend of mine, Yannick Bruynoghe. The Chateau is on your right as you leave the village of Arbre. You can't miss it. It's a large three storey house close to the road."

He told me that I must be doubly careful, as Yannick's step-father was a Belgian General and constantly under the scrutiny of the Germans.

With all of this and more crammed into my mind, I spent an hour or so studying my notes prior to destroying all but the strip maps.

After dinner that night, we checked the bicycle, particularly tyres and chain. I was given a kit of basic tools and a puncture outfit. I hoped I would not have to use them.

Madame Smeyers-Jurion came into my room and we talked for quite a long time. I told her of my home and family, my loneliness. I said that my contact with the Jurion family had, to a large extent, dispelled the feeling of despair and isolation I had suffered two nights before. I also said that I fully understand the extreme risk that the family was taking to help me and for that I would be forever grateful. I gave her my mother's address in Melbourne and she promised to write as soon as it was possible.

I went to bed early so that I could start my ride first thing in the morning, hopefully dodging the soldiers of the Third Reich.

Next morning, Paolo woke me at 6.30am and I was out of bed quickly, uneasily anticipating the day's hazardous ride. I washed at the large pump in the courtyard and even though it was mid-summer, the chilly morning and the icy water provided a refreshing start to the day. Nevertheless, I was glad to get back inside and dress as the farmhands were already about, preparing the draught horses for the day's work.

After a hearty farm breakfast and another check of my bicycle, I was ready to go. I found that my ankles were much improved after the rest and the attention they had been given.

Madame Smeyers-Jurion brought me a parcel of food for the day. "Inside there's meat, cheese and bread, and milk in a bottle. Please be careful." she pleaded. I strapped the parcel on to the bike's carrier.

Monsieur and Madame Jurion waved from inside the farmhouse so as not to make too much of a fuss outside.

The Smeyers boys wished me well but I was sure that they really did not think I would make it. Paolo walked to the gate with me and pointed down the road to the east.

"That's the way you go. Don't forget to stick to our planned route. If you get lost, we can't help you. You'll be alright though. Give my regards to Yannick. Oh yes, you never know, I might see you later." I wondered what he meant.

It was eight o'clock as I rode away from Bonne Esperance, passing Vellereille-les-Brayeux on my right and glanced back towards the gate of the farm. Paolo had gone. I was on my own.

Eighty kilometres to Arbre (more likely ninety, allowing for twists and turns), at 10 kilometres per hour meant that I should arrive around 4 pm, well before dark. I had been told that most of the country I was to ride through was flat.

I soon reached a main road and had to be very careful. This was a much-used route from Binche to the French border and it was certainly busy. Most of the

THE AUTHOR SETS OFF BY BICYCLE ON
HIS JOURNEY CROSS BELGIUM - JULY 1943

traffic was horse-drawn carts and people on bicycles but no soldiers - thank goodness. Nevertheless I rode as fast as I could.

It was only a couple of kilometres to Merbes St. Marie, where I was to turn left on to minor roads all the way to Arbre. Reaching the village, I turned left and as expected, the road was almost free of traffic. Occasionally I passed a horse and cart or a cyclist whom I greeted with a friendly, "bon matin, Monsieur." [Good morning, Sir]. Perhaps I should have said nothing, as my friendliness was not always returned. It was hard for people to exhibit 'joie de vivre' in downtrodden Belgium in 1943. Most were understandably suspicious of strangers, particularly friendly ones.

I rode on for about two hours then, horror upon horror, my front tyre punctured. I reckoned I was about half-way between the villages of Ragnies and Stree. Lucky it was the front wheel because that tyre and tube are easier to remove and repair. In the tool kit was all that I needed to do the job, so I got on with it.

I was just about finished when a German Mercedes staff car came down the road towards me. As it drew near, it slowed down and stopped. It looked as though I was about to be treated to a luxurious ride to a Nazi prison camp in a German staff car. The driver wore the green uniform of a German soldier and seated in the back were two Wehrmacht [Army] officers. One barked at me in the Draconian manner of the master race but I did not understand a word. I held my breath, fearing the worst.

"Thuin, Thuin, imbecile," he yelled at me in French, "ou est Thuin?" [Where is Thuin?] Then I understood. Luckily I had studied my maps well and I knew exactly where Thuin was.

Trying hard to look stupid, I held up ten fingers and pointed along the road to the north. "Dix kilometres par la, monsieur," [Ten kilometres that way, Sir] I mumbled, bowing my head submissively. In my shaken state of mind, I had nearly spoken English again.

A word from the other officer and the vehicle took off with not a word of thanks from any of the Jerries. I could not have cared less. The relief at seeing the back of that car was the greatest. Somehow, miraculously, I had survived my first real face to face encounter with the enemy. Who needed a ride in a Mercedes, anyway?

Spurred on by the fear of another encounter, my crude hand pump filled the flat tyre with air as quick as a flash. Then I was off, my sore ankles pumping pedals like wildfire. Two hours later, after passing Chastres, the road was straight and uncomplicated through to Arbre.

The memory of my encounter with the German army had faded, so naturally, my thoughts turned to the package of food on the carrier behind me. It was time to rest and eat.

Nobody was about so I went into a wheat field, sat down and ate my fill. Judging by the height of the sun, it was about half past twelve. Only half way to Arbre with four hours gone already, there was no way of getting there by 4 o'clock as planned. It would be more like 6 or 7pm so I would have to get a move on.

On my bike again, I reached the Charleroi to Philippeville road. This main highway was one of three between Brussels and Paris and carried much German military traffic to and from France. As I waited to cross, it struck me as strange that there I was, a British airman, watching truckloads of German troops and military paraphernalia go by. One day, I had been concerned with the techniques of flying Lancasters and the next, I was a master evader, dodging the Nazi police. You certainly had to be adaptable to survive during W.W.2. What a life!!

On the other side of the highway, was the last, straight stretch of road to Arbre which was 25 kilometres away.

Three hours later, I turned left at Bioul with just five kilometres to go and still carefully followed Paolo's verbal directions. The road was now very hilly, making cycling most difficult. Having to walk my bike slowly uphill and not trusting myself to make up time by riding fast downhill, I fell further behind. It was dark when, after passing through the village of Arbre, I arrived at the heavy steel spiked gates of Le Chateau de Marteau-Longe.

CHAPTER 5

LE CHATEAU DE MARTEAU-LONGE

THE CHATEAU
PHOTOGRAPHED IN 1943.

The Chateau was a picturesque three-storey mansion standing back about 100 feet from the roadway. It overlooked an 80 or 90 foot circular gravel courtyard with a large central rose garden. There were two lower buildings on either side, the one on the right appearing to be part of the Chateau. The one on the left was apparently a large stable.

I tried to open the heavy steel gates but they were securely locked. I could not find a bell or any other way of gaining attention.

The only thing to do was use my bike as a ladder. I tried to climb over the gates but steel spikes shaped like spears made the climb a case of sticking more than one's neck out. Defeated, I climbed back down to the ground.

Then I saw that the tops of the gate posts were flat, leaving a gap of about one foot between the spears. I climbed up and straddled the fence in the gap. From there it was not too hard to slide down the other side, ensuring that those essential parts of my anatomy remained undamaged.

I was now in the courtyard but the Chateau was blacked out. Even so, I could see a chink of light coming from a second storey window. Maybe that was Yannick Bruynoghe's room. I decided to attract the attention of whoever was behind the chink, rather than alert the whole household by knocking at the front door. I threw pebbles and small stones at the window but it took about five minutes before the light went out and the window opened.

"Qui est la?" [Who is there?] a male voice said.

"Un vieil ami d'ecole de Yannick." [An old school friend of Yannick] I replied as best I could in French.

"Etes-vous Flamand?" [Are you Flemish?] the voice asked. He obviously noticed my unusual accent. I remembered the man in the town square a few days ago and thought that perhaps I had better be careful.

"Oui, monsieur. Yannick est-il la?" [Yes, Sir. Is Yannick there?] I replied.

"Oui. Attendez la," [Yes. Wait there] the voice said.

A few minutes later the front door of the Chateau opened and a young man about my age came down into the courtyard to where I was standing.

"Bienvenue, c'est bon de vous voir apres si longtemps. Entrez et faites connaissance avec ma famille." [Welcome, it is good to see you after so long. Come in and meet my family]

I thought that his greeting was strange as Paolo had arranged my transfer to Yannick, so he must have known who I was. Why speak French? Why so formal? I was soon to find out.

In English, he said quietly, "I am Yannick Bruynoghe. The man that you just spoke to is Italian. He is a servant but has been placed in the Chateau by the Germans to watch my step-father, General Nicod. What did you say to him?"

"Nothing really," I replied, "I told him that I was Flemish. He seemed to believe me."

"That's good. It's alright though," Yannick continued, "you see we pay him more than the Germans, so he only tells enough to satisfy them. Nevertheless there is no point in letting him know too much. Now come inside and meet my family."

"I had to climb the gates. My bike is still outside," I told him.

"Don't worry, I'll get it later," Yannick assured me.

We mounted the steps to the front door of the Chateau and its entrance hall was in keeping with the tenor expected of such a magnificent mansion. With its traditional tiled floor and prominent staircase backed by stained glass windows, this lobby expressed the best of seventeenth century Europe. Later I found the rest of the house to be the same.

As Yannick and I entered, General Emile Nicod and Madame Juliette Nicod-Genicot were waiting to greet me.

"Welcome to the Chateau de Marteau-Longe," the General said, "but why not come into our lounge where it is more private?" His use of the word 'private' did not escape me. The Italian watchdog could well be lurking.

I told them about my bicycle ride from the Abbaye de Bonne Esperance and my brush with the German staff car.

"You were very lucky," Madame Nicod-Genicot observed, "whenever the

GENERAL EMILE NICOD AND MADAM JULIETTE NICOD-GENICOT AT THE FUNERAL OF QUEEN ASTRID - IN 1935

Germans stop anyone they usually ask for identification papers."

Just then a little girl about seven or eight years old came in and ran to the General.

"Voici ma fille Marie-Claire. Dis bonsoir au Monsieur et va vite te coucher, ma cherie." [This is my daughter Marie-Claire] he said in French. [Say goodnight to the gentleman and go quickly to bed, my darling]

"She's very young and if she gets to know too much, she might talk about you at school," Yannick explained, "you know what children are like." After that, I did not see much of little Marie-Claire Nicod.

A man about 30 years old, came into the room and he was introduced by the General. "This is my step-son and Yannick's brother, Doctor Guy Bruynoghe." he said. Doctor Guy shook my hand warmly.

"Could you look at my ankles later," I said, "I sprained them when I landed by parachute and they are still very painful.

"Certainly," Doctor Guy replied, "just as soon as we have finished dinner". A maid had just announced that dinner was being served.

"Can I wash up a little?" I asked, "The journey and climbing your gate have left their mark."

"Of course," said Yannick and showed me to a ground floor washroom.

In the dining room a large table was set formally. I was seated alongside

Yannick with Doctor Guy opposite and General and Madame Nicod at either end. I was certainly the odd one out in this company with my ill-fitting farm clothing more than a little out of place at this table.

After soup, Madame Nicot-Genicot asked me if I had eaten roast goat before.

"Never," I replied.

"If you are willing to try it, you will find that it has the same texture and flavour as lamb," she said. I was willing and I was hungry.

Supported by roast potatoes and peas, the roast goat was delicious. Apple pie and cream followed, then coffee. I thought for a moment that at least some people lived well in occupied Europe. Then I realised that this meal was a special effort just for me. I felt ashamed of my thoughts and was relieved that they had remained unsaid.

After dinner I talked about my parents, my home and my life before the war. Yannick told me that he and Doctor Guy were from a previous marriage of Madame Nicod. Their father, Professor Richard Bruynoghe, had died many years ago.

Doctor Guy inspected my ankles. "No bones broken," he reported, "they'll be right in a couple of days."

Again, as at Bonne Esperance, they told me to keep as low a profile as possible. Even though he was a Belgian general, Monsieur Nicod would still suffer the wrath of the Nazis if I was caught at the Chateau de Marteau-Longe and so would his family.

Later I was shown to my bedroom and after a shower, climbed into bed in borrowed pyjamas. That night I slept like a log.

I woke next morning and lay in bed, lazily thinking how fortunate I had been. Mulling over the events of the last few days and my present situation, I wondered how long it would be before lady luck ran out. I had survived quite a few close shaves, but for the most part she had been on my side. I was convinced that I had come this far because I had not acted furtively and had, for the most part, been openly 'on view'.

My thoughts were interrupted by Yannick knocking on the door.

"It's eight o'clock. Time to get up for breakfast," he called. I used the wash basin in my room, dressed and went down to the dining room where Yannick and Doctor Guy were waiting,

"What will you have for breakfast?" Yannick asked, "we have cereals, toast, bacon and eggs or just bread and cheese. Whatever you wish."

Jokingly I said. "Eggs by the dozen, please." When my plate was brought in, it was covered by three eggs, bacon and slices of toast. I noticed Yannick and Guy were having a simple breakfast of bread and cheese. Was I wolfing their ration of eggs and bacon? How unthinking I had been. I would certainly have to be more considerate in the future.

Just as we were finishing our meal the telephone rang and Yannick answered it. Even though the conversation was in French, I gathered that it was Paolo at the other end.

"He asked if his parcel has arrived," Yannick told me. "I said it had and that it was in the peak of condition. He said he will come over by train tomorrow."

"Isn't travel restricted by the Germans?" I asked.

"Not for students," Yannick replied.

I noticed little Marie-Claire waiting in the hall and Doctor Guy got up and taking her by the hand, went outside.

"Guy is taking her to school," Yannick said, "she attends the Monastery de Burnot just down the road,"

We spent the rest of the morning discussing the next move.

"It's Tuesday today," Yannick said finally, "I know there are organisations that can arrange for people to get out of Europe through Spain or Switzerland. Spain then Portugal is best because Switzerland interns foreigners, although I have heard that it's not a bad spot to sit out the war." He smiled. "I will talk to my priest after Mass next Sunday. Anyway let's see what Paolo thinks tomorrow."

General and Madame Nicod joined us for lunch and we spent the afternoon and evening talking about the war and conditions in Belgium compared with those in England. They appeared very interested in Australia and why my comrades and I had travelled so far, while Australia is in danger from the Japanese.

"I suppose that in the long run we all do what we are told," I responded.

Next morning, by way of apologising for the previous day's thoughtlessness, I chose a continental breakfast.

"We're going to move you again," Yannick announced after we finished, "but not very far this time. Paolo and I did a lot of camping before the war, so we have all the equipment necessary to hide you in the woods nearby. "You see," he continued, "it's going to take awhile to contact the underground and it's much too risky for you to stay at the Chateau. We have regular check visits from the Germans, even at breakfast time. They like eggs too," he said with a wily grin. "Anyway, Paolo should be here soon. Let's see what he thinks."

Paolo arrived at about 11am and was keen to hear about my bicycle trip across Belgium, so I went over it all again.

"Fancy a German staff car stopping and talking to you," he said, intrigued, "they usually ask for papers."

"I know," I replied, "that's what Madame Nicod said. They seemed to be in too much of a hurry to worry about papers."

"Which reminds me," Paolo said, "we had a dreadful shock yesterday. About midday, a big Mercedes sedan with Nazi flags and emblems all over it and a German officer sitting in the back, drove into the courtyard of Bonne Esperance. "Our first thoughts were that you had been captured and identified with us. Or maybe one of the farmhands had talked. It was too much of a coincidence for you to leave one day and the Germans visit us the next."

Paolo continued, "The driver got out of the car and smartly ran around to open the back door to let his officer out. He was a Major and as he approached us, we recognised him as a regular visitor from Binche. He had come for his monthly hand-out of farm produce." Paolo laughed. "To his surprise, on this occasion we welcomed him with open arms."

Yannick told Paolo of the decision to move me into the woods. "We think it would be wise to erect a tent on the hill behind the Chateau. We could take it in turns keeping our comrade from the skies company. That is so long as you can stay for awhile."

"As long as you like," volunteered Paolo.

That night, after getting the camping equipment together and checking it, the three of us sat around listening to records. Yannick was a jazz fiend and a keen follower of the "Hot Club of France". He had hundreds of records and a fine amplifier. Like the teenagers we were, we spent a couple of happy hours sheltered from the reality of 1943 by an umbrella of music. For the moment the war and "les sales Boches" were far, far away.

At 10 am the next day, on the 1st July, the three of us, each burdened with his share of camping paraphernalia, left the Chateau to establish a bivouac that was to be my hiding-place for three long weeks.

We passed through a well-tended vegetable garden at the rear of the Chateau, then entered the forest on the other side of the road that wound its way back to the village of Arbre. We hauled our loads up a thickly wooded, steep hill for about one hundred yards.

The site Yannick chose to pitch the tent was strewn with large rocks. It had good treetop protection from inquisitive aircraft and thick under-growth ensured that we would not be seen from ground level. About 12 o'clock we were feeling peckish.

"I'll go down and get something to eat," volunteered Yannick.

By the time he got back, Paolo and I had finished putting everything into

THE AUTHOR AT THE CAMPSITE NEAR
THE VILLAGE OF ARBRE IN JULY 1943

place and were lying back, lazily enjoying the woods around us and the sun filtering through the canopy overhead.

"You two obviously don't think there's a war on," Yannick said, bringing us both back to reality. "Let's eat and then discuss how we'll operate from now on."

After we had finished eating, Yannick said. "I've brought enough food to last until morning. I'll go down to the Chateau and stay there tonight, leaving Paolo up here. Tomorrow Paolo can go down for supplies and I'll stay up here for the day and so on. OK?"

"That's alright," I said, "but if baskets of food are prepared in the Chateau's kitchen each day, carried across the road and up into the woods, won't the servants, particularly the Italian, start to wonder why? It might not be anyone from the Chateau who gives us away - someone that lives around here might get curious."

"You're right," Yannick responded a little angrily, "but what else can we do? I know there are risks. But first we have to hide you, and second we have to feed you. We can't avoid the possibility of being spotted. All we can do is minimise the risk by being as careful as possible."

I felt a little ashamed for questioning the arrangement. Both Paolo and Yannick knew how dangerous their position was. They also knew that the whole Nicod/Bruynoghe family was at risk. And for that matter, so was the family at Bonne Esperance. If caught, I would be OK as I would go to a Prisoner of War camp. They might well be shot and their families sent to concentration camps. After all, I was the hot potato, not them. If I was not there they would be going about their daily tasks without fear of danger.

From then on I shut up, leaving my future in their hands. They knew what they were doing.

On Saturday, Paolo brought up three bottles of beer, "to wish our campsite good fortune." he said.

We included these with our midday meal, making the occasion a most joyful one. Even though there was still an underlying sense of apprehension, by mid-afternoon our bivouac seemed a remarkably carefree place, a feeling enthusiastically shared by my

THE AUTHOR AND PAOLO SHARING A MEAL AT THE SECRET CAMP-SITE

happy companions.

Just before he left for the night, Yannick promised that after Mass at the Monastery de Burnot the following morning, he would take the Superieur, Father Balthasar, aside and tell him about me. "I suspect that there have been other occasions when Father has been of help to people such as you," Yannick confided.

"How about I come to church with you," I said brightly, "I'd like to meet Father."

"Too dangerous," Yannick said quickly, "most services are watched by the German police."

Next day Yannick brought the news that although he could not repeat exactly what was said, nevertheless Father Balthasar had set wheels in motion and that we should have more news in a week or so.

"That long!" I exclaimed and then bit my tongue. I realised that I was pushing too hard.

"It will take time," Paolo interrupted, "You will have to be patient. You don't find members of the resistance walking along the street with labels hanging around their necks, you know."

Things simmered down a little when Yannick produced a camera. He took a number of photos of the camp, of me cheerfully holding up an empty beer bottle from yesterday, of Paolo and of himself. He promised that these would be sent on to my mother after the war. In the long run, I had to admit that our weekend had been pretty successful.

The following week was uneventful. My companion for each day and I, sat around reading boring old English books, or French magazines where only the pictures were intelligible to me.

On one occasion an old woodsman approached and Paolo greeted him in French. They chatted for a time, then the old man left.

"What did you tell him?" I asked.

"I told him we are students from a local college," Paolo replied. "We are on a survival project to camp out for a week and then report to our class of our experiences. He accepted that and has gone on his way."

The following Sunday, Yannick came back from Mass and broke the news that I was to be moved again. "It won't be until Friday or Saturday," he said, "but the resistance has been contacted and they are willing to help you." It seemed that the wheels, set in motion last week, were now turning a little quicker. Knowing that the next stage of my evasion was not far away, made the week drag by slowly.

Yannick and I did have one scare. On Tuesday afternoon, we heard the sound of an engine, then saw an aircraft coming low over the hill towards us. I recognised it as a Fieseler Storch, a flimsy skeleton of an aircraft used by the German army, mostly as a spotter 'plane. This one seemed to be either patrolling the area or possibly transporting some high ranking Nazi officer hither, thither and yon. Yannick and I dived into the tent and I won by a short head.

The Storch circled once then flew on. As it did not come back, I guessed the pilot had not seen us or thought we were not worth worrying about. Ten minutes later, we cautiously emerged from the tent.

On Saturday morning the 17th July, Paolo and I heard Yannick coming up the hill towards us.

"Well, this is it," he said as he approached. "I'm to take you to the monastery now." Even though I had known for a week that I would soon have to leave our camp and my two comrades, for just a moment I was taken by surprise. Then, as I shook Paolo's hand, a deep sense of gratitude overcame me. The risks he and his family in Bonne Esperance had been willing to take on my behalf, would never be forgotten.

I gathered up my few belongings and followed Yannick down the hill away from our campsite and away from Paolo. As we passed the gates of the Chateau de Marteau Longe, I was reminded of the protection so freely offered by the Nicod/Bruynoghe family over the past three weeks and of the dire risks they too had been willing to take on my behalf.

We walked half a mile to the Monastery de Burnot and as we approached, a door opened and I entered.

I looked back for Yannick but he was gone and I had not even said goodbye. Inside the monastery, a monk beckoned me to follow him and led me into a room where a priest was sitting behind a desk. In faltering English, the priest told me that he was Father Henri Balthazar, Superieur of the monastery and then

THE MONASTERY DE BURNOT ARBRE
AS IT WAS IN 1975.

introduced my guide as Brother Jacques. Father Balthazar went on to say that Brother Jacques would look after me whilst I was their guest and that I would be with them for one or two days. Should I need to talk to him at any time, I only had to ask.

Brother Jacques then took me to a small cell-like bed room. His English was even worse than my French, so conversation was most difficult. However, he indicated that, for security reasons, I would have to eat in my room. Should I want anything at any time, day or night, I was to press a bell push near the door. Right now he would get me some books to read.

He went away, but was soon back with a scant midday meal and three books written in French. I got through the meal but not the books. There were no pictures!

I spent two lonely days and nights in that small room, not knowing what was to happen to me next. Being limited to monosyllabic conversation with Brother Jacques and then solitude and silence for long periods, was distressing, even with a friendly custodian. Had he been a belligerent, it would have been terrifying. I wondered if I was ever to find out.

Many years later, my interest in the Monastery de Burnot was re-kindled when I read an article sent to me from Europe, describing some of their activities during the Second World War. It seems that I was not the only evader who was sheltered at the monastery. In addition, refugees, dissidents, resistance members, non-cooperative students, Jews and escaping allied P.O.W.'s were also given sanctuary. The Fathers even helped the American troops as they advanced towards the Meuse river in 1944. They revealed pockets of German resistance and established a temporary hospital for both civilian and military wounded.

Earlier Father Balthazar and a previous Superieur, Father Godeau, had been summoned before the German Security Police in Charleroi. Both Fathers were accused of being enemies of the German Reich, of plotting vengeance, of encouraging non-cooperation amongst the local population and distributing "Free Belgium", an underground newspaper. After prolonged interrogation, Father Godeau was incarcerated in Charleroi prison and Father Balthazar was allowed to return to Burnot alone.

Eventually Father Godeau was taken before the German Council of War in the Law Courts at Namur and sentenced to eight months prison. He suffered the horrors of the concentration camps of Buchenwald, Varsovia and Dachau, and did not return to Burnot until the war ended.

In the same way, most of the abbeys, monasteries and convents of occupied Europe protected patriots and escaping allied military personnel from the Nazis.

Many died for their actions.

Lest we forget.

RESISTANCE

Extrait d'un journal régional :

« Il nous revient que durant cette guerre, le couvent de Burnot hébergea de nombreux ouvriers réfractaires, des juifs, des prisonniers anglais échappés des camps allemands, ainsi qu'un pilote américain de la Royal Australian Air Force. Le Supérieur de ce couvent faisait en outre partie de diverses organisations alliées de renseignement. A l'occasion de fêtes qui viennent d'être célébrées à Rivière, il était bon de signaler l'activité patriotique de cet établissement qui fait honneur à la région. »

Voici quelques faits :

Le 23 mars 1942, le Père Godeau et le Père Balthasar, Recteur à cette époque, sont convoqués pour 9 h. 30 à la Sicherheitspolizei à Charleroi. Tous deux subissent un interrogatoire serré pendant 2 heures et demie. Immédiatement après, le Père Godeau est conduit à la prison de Charleroi et le Père Balthasar rentre seul au Juvénat. Deux lettres anonymes datant l'une du 15 décembre 1941 et l'autre du 9 février 1942 dénoncent les PP. Godeau et Balthasart comme adversaires des Allemands. Ils sont accusés de nourrir des projets de vengeances, d'inciter la population à ne pas livrer les cuivres, d'accueillir et de propager « La Libre Belgique » et de recevoir du Grand Duché de Luxembourg des missives discutant l'action de la Gestapo. Le 8 avril, le Père Balthasar est convoqué au tribunal allemand pour subir un nouvel interrogatoire. Le 21 avril, à 9 h., le Père Godeau passe le conseil de guerre au Palais de Justice de Namur, et est condamné à huit mois de prison. Mais cette peine se prolongera jusqu'à la libération dans les souffrances des camps de concentration de Buchenwald, Varsovie et Dachau.

L'aide aux alliés.

En juin 1943, nous gardons quinze jours le sergent pilote Gordon Stooke de la Royal Australian Air Force, un courageux pilote de vingt ans qui, après avoir effectué un raid de bombardement sur Wuppertal, vit son appareil atteint par la D. C. A. ennemie. Il donna ordre à ses coéquipiers de descendre en parachute, sauta lui-même dans le vide et vit son appareil s'écraser en flammes. Après bien des dangers en territoire occupé par l'ennemi, il trouva un refuge sûr au Juvénat.

Le Père Recteur entra immédiatement en communication avec la ligue pour le rapatriement des aviateurs alliés. La Comtesse de B... de Namur lui fut d'un grand secours. Par une matinée ensoleillée, une voiture s'arrêta devant la porte, un mot de passe et le pilote disparut. Dans une lettre il annonça au P. Recteur, que deux hommes de son équipage étaient déjà repartis pour la Grande-Bretagne, un troisième devait suivre. Des trois autres, deux furent faits prisonniers et le troisième était hospitalisé pour une fracture.

AN EXTRACT FROM THE 1945 EDITION OF THE JOURNAL 'RESISTANCE' MENTIONING THE AUTHOR'S ACTIVITIES IN BELGIUM.

CHAPTER 6

LE CAPITAINE

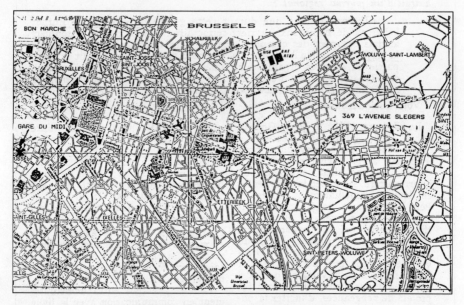

THE AREA OF BRUSSELS BETWEEN THE
RAILWAY STATION AND AVENUE SLEGERS

At about 10am on Monday 19th July, Father Balthazar came to my room to tell me that a car from the Belgian resistance had arrived. Parked outside the Monastery was a small sedan driven by a woman, with another sitting in the back.

As I climbed into the front passenger seat, I was just a little nervous and unhappy about parting with my Belgian protectors and the haven they had provided. I was also uneasy to be out in the open with strangers, exposed once more. But my apprehension did not last long.

The closing of the car door was a signal to the driver to be off. We sped down the road towards the town of Reviere and then north towards Namur.

"My name is Annie," the driver told me. Even though she spoke with a heavy accent, her English was good. "My friend in the back is Voletta." Annie was about 35 years old, with black hair and eyes and her black beret enhanced her southern European complexion. As she drove, I notice a tattoo on her wrist.

She chatted amicably on. "We know all about you," she told me, "you were the pilot of a Lancaster bomber from 460 Squadron, shot down a month ago and you are Australian." I was puzzled how she knew all this.

"How did you find that out?" I asked her.

"We have our ways," she replied. "I'm taking you to Brussels where there are others like you, who need help to get out of Europe." She said nothing about how this was to be done, only that all will be revealed by a 'wonderful man' who had helped hundreds of other British and American airmen.

The nonchalant attitude of these two women, along with their constant chatter, lulled me into a sense of security. Even so, I was intrigued by the way Annie drove the car at speed, particularly through the streets of Brussels. There were German soldiers everywhere and no doubt, Nazi security police as well. I found this devil-may-care attitude a little curious.

At midday, we arrived at 369 Avenue Sleghers, Woluwe, Brussels. It was a block of flats and I was led up to the third floor. The lounge room had been turned into a dormitory where half a dozen men were lying on sleeping bags, reading or yarning among themselves. Four were dressed in civilian clothes, the other two still wore R.A.F. battledress, without insignias.

As I entered the room, they all stopped whatever they were doing and looked up at me. Two of them either could not or would not speak English so I thought it best to leave them alone. The other two, dressed in civvies, were R.A.F. officers and three of the airmen were gunners. They had all been shot down by fighters and did not know what had happened to the rest of their crews. Their stories were similar; aircraft severely damaged; one had lost most of its port wing; on fire and out of control. Overwhelming terror and peril had touched off unrestrained attempts to survive. Little room for heroism.

The fourth, a navigator, believed that at least two of his crew were alive as the bomb aimer and engineer had jumped before him. The aircraft had been damaged by flak over Gelsenkirchen on the 9-10th July and it suddenly went out of control somewhere east of Antwerp. He did not know what had happened to his pilot or the rest of his crew.

I told them my story, carefully omitting names and places. They were surprised that I had survived for a month without being taken by the Germans. Despite the circumstances, it was good to be back amongst my peers and 'chewing the fat'.

The next morning, I met the 'wonderful man' acclaimed by Annie on our way to Brussels the day before. She introduced him as 'le Capitaine.' He arrived at the flat with another candidate for an urgent trip to Spain.

This evader proved to be a German Priest, Pater Franz, whose anti-Nazi outbursts had hardly endeared him to Der Fuhrer. The Captain was a slight man, about 50 years old with stiffly-combed black hair, turning grey at the temples. He was wearing gloves and a trench-coat and later, I noticed that he had lost the little finger of his right hand.

"Welcome to the new arrivals." He spoke with an American accent. "All your worries are over now. Soon you will be with the British authorities in Spain. But first we have a few things to do in Brussels to prepare you for the trip. In the meantime, relax and enjoy yourself as best you can. I know it's not easy being confined in this flat but try to make the most of it."

Smiling, he approached me and shook my hand. "How do you do," he said, "I believe you are Australian. We had two of your countrymen pass through here the other day." He called to Annie. "What were the names of the two Australians?"

"Craven and Conklin," she replied, "and there was an Englishman with them, Toohig." I was so relieved that it must have shown.

"Your crew, obviously," the Captain said, "what are the names of the others?" Now I had a dilemma. It had been drilled into us that 'mum's the word' under all circumstances. On the other hand, why should I mistrust the very man who was about to deliver me from the iron fist of the Hun.

"I don't know what's happened to them," I said evasively, "I had not heard of Craven, Conklin and Toohig until Annie mentioned their names a few moments ago." I felt pretty silly trying to be smart with the Captain but he seemed to accept what I had said and did not ask me any more questions.

Some time later, Clarrie Craven told me that soon after he had landed by parachute, he met Dennis Toohig by chance. They decided to stay together and walk to Spain, 600 miles away. At dawn, they crawled into a wheat field and fitfully slept the day away. Soaked to the skin, hungry and thirsty, they continued on for three days, hiding by day and walking by night.

By the 28th June, they were badly in need of help and contacted a farming family who took them to the local Priest, Father Jos Hanuset - their conversation interpreted by a brave little Belgian schoolgirl. Taken to a Convent near Liege, they spent two nights in the care of the Nuns of le Maison du Sacre Coeur and the good Priest, Father Cardyn. Next day they were picked up by the Captain and taken to this same flat in Brussels. A coincidence, or was there a connection?

That evening, the Captain announced that the following morning we were to be photographed for bogus passports. "The younger men will be described as Flemish students and the older men as their tutors," he said. "I know that you're all anxious about your escape route to Spain, but I'll tell you of that later. Now for the photographs. Tomorrow we'll go to a large Emporium in Brussels where there's a booth for taking identification card photographs. Nothing unusual about that. They're busy these days, because identity cards are compulsory in Belgium. There are eight of you, so the first two will come with me in my car. Three more will follow half an hour later, driven by Annie. The last three, half an hour after that, with Voletta.

"I want to get it over quickly with no delays," he went on, "We'll leave early before there are too many people in the Emporium. Now are there any questions?"

"What about clothes?" one of the R.A.F. men asked. "Two of us are still wearing our uniforms."

"That's taken care of. We have plenty of civvy clothes here," the Captain said. "You can try them on now, if you wish." He departed, leaving us merrily fighting over a bundle of rather drab hand-me-downs. I stayed with the clothes Paolo had given me back at Bonne Esperance. After a brushing-up and an ironing they were not too bad.

Next morning, I found that I was to go with the second group, driven by Annie. So at about 9.30am, three of us climbed into her car and left Avenue

Sleghers. As planned, the Captain, with his two passengers, had gone on before us. We drove along a wide avenue, passing a magnificent monument not unlike pictures I had seen of the Arc de Triomphe in Paris. Later I learnt that it was the Cinquentenaire.

Because there was little fuel for private use, most traffic in the city of Brussels was military. I wondered how the Captain and his band got away with such open use of their cars, as checks were constantly being made on private vehicles by the German police. Still, who was I to reason why?

Soon we stopped outside a large retail store.

"Bon Marche," Annie told us.

Towards the rear of the ground floor was a booth where each of us in turn had his photograph taken. Looking around while waiting for the films to be developed, I noticed how dull and uninteresting the store was. There was very little offered for sale and I was told that even the few goods available were of low quality and severely rationed. Foodstuffs were also rationed and the selection on the shelves was restricted, even for those who had ration tickets. Europe was surviving, but hungry, under the New Order of the Third Reich.

We collected our developed photos and started back to the flat in Annie's car. Apparently there was an incident of some sort on the Boulevard along which we had come, so we used another route for our return. As we passed through a park, I saw a large building not unlike Buckingham Palace in London. Annie told me that it was the Palais du Roi.

Soon we were back at 369 Avenue Sleghers critically comparing photographs and wondering how we had got away with the morning's outing. The Captain took our photographs to one of the resistance's graphic artists to prepare the bogus passports. He said they should be ready by the weekend.

Four more tedious days passed in that Brussels flat and I was getting a little edgy. One way or another, I had been confined for over a month and constant tension under restraint was becoming a little hard to handle.

Meanwhile I had become friendly with the two tight-lipped men in civilian clothes. It turned out that before joining the resistance, they were Dutch policemen. They had been involved in a shooting affray with the German army with casualties on both sides. A German soldier had since died from his wounds, so they had to get out of Europe, fast.

On Sunday evening the 25th July, the Captain handed out our passports, announcing that tomorrow we were off to Paris. He spelt out a few rules, "You are going by train. Remember, you are Flemish students and the two Dutchmen and Father Franz are your Tutors. So also is the guide accompanying you. His name is Pierre and he will be changed when you reach Paris. At all times do exactly what your guides tell you. Don't speak English unless you have to and keep a low profile at all times. We'll pick you up at 9 o'clock in the morning and drive you to the Gare du Midi. All the best for your trip to Spain," he said as he left the flat.

With the excitement of it all, sleep was difficult that night.

We left the flat next day at exactly 9.00am as planned, arriving at the Gare du Midi at 9.20am. The Paris train was ready so we climbed on board and into a compartment reserved for us. The guide Pierre was introduced and the Captain, Annie and Voletta left us in his care.

Waiting for the train to leave, I had time to look around and take stock. The eight of us filled a first class compartment, so there was no room for anyone else. Watching the passengers as they boarded the train, I was a little taken aback to see a group of German Army officers get on. Until then, most passengers looked like civilian officials or maybe students. I was disturbed by the openness of it all and the ease with which we were carrying out our deception. It all seemed too simple, too smooth. I would have expected a more clandestine, cloak-and-dagger operation. I was not sure whether to be disappointed or alarmed. Anyway there was not much I could do about it and surely I must not forget that the Captain was a 'wonderful man' who had helped hundreds escape Hitler's hordes.

A high-pitched whistle, characteristic of all French steam engines, then a huff and a puff followed by a jerk and a jolt and we were on our way to Paris. Before long we were steaming through the tranquil Belgian countryside. Yellowish-brown wheat fields gave way to green pasture, alternating, until we noisily passed by a stone cottaged village. No sign of hostility here, in an area that had been dubbed "the Battleground of Europe". Almost every war from Waterloo, to W.W.1 and its bloody trenches and to the recent German blitzkrieg into France, had been fought here. And there would be more battles to come, no doubt.

We had just reached the small township of Halle, when a French conductor came by collecting tickets. Pierre already had everything under control. Handing our tickets to the conductor, he pointed us out as his students. That was all there was to it. The cancelled stubs were given back to Pierre and we sat back and enjoyed more of the passing countryside, relieved that the conductor apparently suspected nothing.

The train came to a halt in woods from time to time. Perhaps the driver was avoiding strafing Spitfires and Mosquitos. If so, I prayed that any attacks against this train would be unsuccessful on this occasion.

After leaving Braine-le-Comte, Pierre mentioned that the train would stop for about ten minutes at Mons, just before crossing the French/Belgian border.

"You've no need to worry," he said, "just relax, sit calmly and I'll make sure that no one comes near you."

Waiting in that train at Mons station, I remembered that a month ago, at Gembloux, I had chosen this well known First World War town as my Checkpoint '1'.

"Oh well, better to be here late than never." I thought.

As the train gathered way out of Mons, Pierre told us that we were approaching the Belgian/French border.

"When we stop," he explained, "a French customs officer and a German immigration officer will inspect the train. The German is in our pay so his inspection of your documents will be a pretence. The customs officer will follow his lead, so all will be well. Now hand me your passports."

It all seemed rather fanciful to me. I was glad that I had kept my dog tags, so that I could identify myself should the Captain's grand plan go astray.

A whistle and the grind of brakes announced our arrival at the Douane Francaise. Just as Pierre had predicted, two officers, one German and one French, went from compartment to compartment examining everyone's papers and luggage. When it was our turn, the German took our passports from Pierre, glanced through them and with a sly grin, handed them back.

Twenty minutes later, near the township of Maubeuge, France, we were given ample proof that truth is stranger than fiction. Pierre announced that there were two tables reserved for us in the dining car. I could not believe it. Here were eight fearful and bewildered evaders of Nazi concentration and prison camps about to openly stroll into the dining car of the Bruxelles/Paris express. We were to lunch with ranking officers of the S.S., the Wehrmacht and in all probability, Gestapo agents and French collaborators. Either the resistance believed, as I did a month ago, that furtive behaviour was more conspicuous than audacity or we were the victims of the greatest "con" this side of Troy.

Obediently we filed in, brushed past the enemy and sat down at allotted tables. We ate silently from a set menu of acceptable food, washed down with an appropriate beverage. To Pierre's credit, we were making use of the dining car during the last sitting, so there were few diners left to pry into our whys and wherefores.

At about 3.30pm we came to the outskirts of not-so-gay Paris and half an hour later, our train pulled into the Gare du Nord.

Pierre reminded us that, as arranged, his responsibility had ended and his replacement would meet us at the station. Sure enough, our new guide was waiting just past the exit gates and was introduced by Pierre as Henri. Pierre wished us 'bon voyage' for our trip to Spain and quickly left.

"We now have a half-hour journey on the Metro," Henri said. "We're booked into a hotel at the Place d'Italie for the night. I warn you that it's imperative that we keep together at all times. If any one of you becomes separated, you will have no chance of avoiding the Germans in Paris. Here the German police are many and they don't take kindly to evaders, especially if they're in civilian clothes."

We boarded the Metro at Gare du Nord. It seemed that even during the German occupation, homeward bound commuters made the Paris underground very busy at that time of day. We stood all the way and although we stopped often, the only two station names I recognised, were Republique and Bastille. We arrived at Place d'Italie at 4.45pm.

Henri herded us off the train and out of the station. A short walk along a large boulevard and then down a side street and we arrived at the Hotel du Grand. Grand by name it may have been but by the look of it, grand this hotel was not. It was dirty and the rooms were small and stuffy.

"Seats are reserved for us on tomorrow's train to Bordeaux," Henri told us. "The station is about 20 minutes walk from here. The train leaves at 10.00am, so you must be up for breakfast by 7.30am."

I was surprised to learn that we were to eat out that night, with a nearby restaurant booked for 6.00pm. At the appointed hour, we were called together and walked a block away to a secluded tavern, where the food was reasonable considering severe rationing in Paris. I tried les Pattes de Grenouille (Frogs legs) but declined les Escargots (Snails). As on the train, le vin de Bordeaux was taken with gusto. Mindful of tomorrow's destination of Bordeaux, this celebration was taken as an omen - favourable of course.

By 9.30pm we were back in our rooms at the Hotel du Grand, settling in for the night. For me, sleep was out of the question as I could not come to terms with the over-confident, off-hand manner in which we had been managed over the last week. How was it that the Captain could drive three private cars around petrol-starved Belgium and not be picked up by the police? How had we got away with a journey to Paris on a train carrying many German army officers? How had we been able to pass German immigration at the border? What about that incredible lunch in the dining car? And there were many other implausible incidents as well.

If the Captain's organisation was corrupt, then it appeared that all was lost. Even if I evaded the 'evaders', my chance of deliverance from occupied Paris and then France, was marginal.

On the other hand if the Captain was bona-fide, then by separating from the group, I would surely miss my opportunity of reaching Spain. My destiny was dictated by percentages. They seemed to favour following Henri.

Next morning, I felt as though I might have enjoyed too much vin de Bordeaux the night before but it is more likely that my thick head was due to having only had about two hours restless sleep.

I still felt suspicious of our guides and for that matter, the whole DeZitter organisation. Something had to be wrong!!

We ate a scanty continental breakfast and by 8.45am, we were on our way to the Gare d'Austerlitz and a train to Bordeau. Crossing the Place d'Italie, we started our twenty-minute walk on the left-hand side of the Boulevard de l'Hopital. Cautiously, maybe even defensively, I hung back from the group a little but Henri ordered me to close up.

Suddenly those in front of me were set upon by half a dozen men in civilian clothes, yelling and brandishing machine guns. I saw one of the Dutchmen go down from a fierce blow to his head with the butt of a gun. One of our attackers came at me and violently jabbed the barrel of his machine gun hard into my stomach. As I turned defensively, he hammered it just as viciously into my back. In agony now, I became aware of guttural bellows of menace and abuse from my attacker.

"Hande hoch, schweinhund, schnell, schnell," [Hands up, pig-dog, quickly, quickly] he screamed.

I could not understand a word he said but I knew what he wanted. I followed the lead set by my companions and grabbed for the sky, with the Hun's gun barrel still painfully boring itself deep into my back. I was lucky to be still on my feet as two more of my comrades had been knocked down by blows to the head and kicked unmercifully.

Knowing that a quick and certain death was only a shaky trigger-finger away, was terrifying. Only the unfortunate few who have experienced the terminal menace of a loaded machine gun aimed at them in anger, know of the abject fear

GESTAPO HEADQUARTERS AT 80-84 AVENUE FOCH
AS IT LOOKED IN 1990.

and the dreadful feeling of finality it engenders. The thought that the gun being shoved so violently into my back, could go off accidentally, even if the unconcerned character at the butt end did not intend it, was petrifying. Ending up a bloody mess on a Paris pavement was a possibility not to be contemplated.

Later it was whispered that we had been captured by the infamous Nazi S.D. (Sicherheitsdienst - Security Service) of the S.S. (Schutzstaffel - Protection Corps). It was obvious they had been waiting for us.

They were to be treated with caution because such had been their training and with their daily involvement in the arrest of dissidents and antagonists, that these dedicated Nazis were insensible and callous.

We were shoved unceremoniously into a waiting bus, Henri included, with the S.D. sitting opposite. Without delay we set forth for who-knows-where with our captors still aiming their cocked machine guns at our midriffs. High hopes had been transformed into deep despair in a matter of a few minutes. While we sat statue-still and upright, the S.D. chatted and laughed among themselves. For about a quarter of an hour we were driven west across Paris and as we passed over the Seine River on the Pont de Bir Hakeim, I noticed the Eiffel Tower to our right.

Soon we arrived at Gestapo headquarters at 80-84 Avenue Foch. I would have cheerfully walked to Hell and back if my watchdog had only stopped ramming the barrel of his gun into my pulverised back. He kept jabbing and by the time we reached an ante-room on the first floor, I was close to vomiting with pain. Even so I made a great effort not to show it. It is amazing how personal pride and native defiance can surface to cover agony and dread.

Watched over by two menacing S.D. guards, we waited anxiously in the ante-room for interrogation by the Gestapo. Our erstwhile guide Henri had disappeared. It seemed that money-grabbing Henri, in league with the Gestapo, was a weak link in the chain of agents attempting to deliver us to Spain. At least, we thought, it showed that the Captain and his crew were bona fide. We had not been fooled by them and they had nothing to do with our new unhappy situation. Not so.

Much later, I discovered that it was not just greedy Henri but the whole organisation that was phoney and in the pay of the Gestapo. Prosper-Valere de Zitter (le Capitaine) was born in Passchendaele on the 19th September, 1893. An automobile dealer, he was married but divorced by his wife, Germaine Prince. Arrested for a serious offence against a woman, he spent six years in a Belgian prison and later went to Canada where he learned to speak English. Consequently he had a North American accent. In 1938 he returned to Belgium and by 1940 had become an agent of the German Gestapo. During that time he was also known as Jack Kilarine, Herbert Call, le Capitaine Tom, le Capitaine Willy Neper, le Capitaine Jackson, le Major Willy and by other aliases.

His mistress, Florentine-Leonarda-Maria-Louisa Giralt, was born in Barcelona in 1904, was married and had one son. She too, was an agent of the Gestapo and used the names Anny, Annie, Flore, Mariette, Voletta, Marlier, etc. She was known to have worked with traitors other than de Zitter. One named Janssens was in reality Schultz of the Gestapo. She was the chatty woman who had driven me from the Monastery de Burnot to Brussels.

De Zitter and Giralt used three properties in Brussels as bases for their infamy. They were paid blood money by the Gestapo for each fugitive that they collected. The most likely person that a desperate evader would contact was a Priest, so de Zitter made it known among the clergy that he had a well-organised chain of guides through to Spain. Convinced, many a loyal churchman, in good faith, provided de Zitter with a constant supply of unsuspecting runaways.

Following their preparation in Brussels and then a train ride, freedom-seekers were handed over to the waiting Gestapo in Paris. This was to make sure that innocent Belgian patriots would never know the fate of the evaders that they had so gallantly helped.

It has been suggested that thousands of people had passed through le Capitaine's organisation. This large number is unlikely but it is certain that due to de Zitter's efforts, many hundreds of unfortunates were taken by the Gestapo and ended up in prison camps or died in concentration camps.

Once his deception was discovered, many unsuccessful attempts were made on de Zitter's life by the Belgian resistance. This 'Wonderful man' and the traitress Giralt were captured in 1945, tried and put to death by a Belgian firing squad.

DE ZITTER, Prosper-Valère, né à Passchendaele (Fl. Occ.), le 19-9-1893, commerçant, courtier en automobiles, divorcé de PRINCE, Germaine.

Se fait passer pour KILARINE, Jack, Canadien ; CALL, Herbert, aviateur canadien, dont il possède le passeport ; WILLIAMS, né à Londres ; le capitaine TOM ; le capitaine NEPER, Willy ; le capitaine JACKSON ; le major WILLY, etc., etc.

Parle bien l'anglais, a vécu treize ans en Amérique.

Parle le français avec un léger accent.

Age apparent : 50 ans, bonne taille moyenne, assez mince, yeux bleus striés de brun ; cheveux initialement blonds, ensuite grisonnants, actuellement bruns ; a parfois des lunettes (différents genres).

Il lui manque deux phalanges à l'auriculaire de la main droite mais porte généralement des gants pour cacher cette infirmité ; ses cheveux sont plaqués et peignés en arrière ; il se laisse parfois pousser une petite moustache noire ; il a souvent l'insigne de la COFAC à la boutonnière.

Est sans domicile fixe, voir ci-après endroits fréquentés.

Dangereux repris de justice, devrait purger six ans de prison pour les autorités belges. Agent de la Gestapo du groupe 46 depuis 1940, possède sa carte en ce sens.

Fait usage des voitures belges : 68.487, 433.835 et 160.615 (C. C.).

GIRALT, Florentine-Léonarda-Maria-Louisa, épouse DINGS, Paul-Stéphan, née à Barcelone, le 21-6-1904 ; son mari est né à Tagelen (Limbourg hollandais), le 24-10-1892 ; a un fils, Serge, né .. Etterbeek, le 29-3-1930.

Paraît plus jeune que son âge réel (30 ans environ), jolie, cheveux noirs, généralement coiffés plats, yeux noirs, teint basané, léger tatouage à un poignet, bonne taille moyenne, nez pointu, menton légèrement en galoche.

Se fait passer pour un agent de l'I. S. et se dit en mesure d'obtenir des messages à la B. B. C. sous le nom de CHEVAL-DE-BOIS.

S'est introduite dans les organisations patriotiques sous les noms de ANNY, ANNIE, FLORE, MARIETTE, VIOLETTA, MARLIER, etc., etc.

Travaille en collaboration avec les traîtres NOOTENS, Jean ; ANCIAUX, Jules ; GOSSELIN, Roger ; MARLIER, Anne ; et un nommé JANSSENS, qui, en réalité, est le nommé STHULZ, de la Gestapo, etc.

Son adresse est : 27, avenue Léon Van Dromme, à Auderghem.

Entre autres endroits ,le couple DE ZITTER-GIRALT fréquente le nº 3 de l'avenue Messidor, Uccle ; le nº 369 de l'avenue Sleghers, Woluwe ; le nº 7 ou le nº 9 du boulevard Saint-Michel, Bruxelles, etc.

UN COUPLE DE SALOPARDS! [A PAIR OF BASTARDS]

"Un couple de salopards!" [A pair of bastards] and I had the misfortune of being involved with both of them.

The first to be taken for interrogation were the two Dutchmen. Remembering that they had been involved in gun battles with German soldiers in Holland, I expected that they were in for a pretty rough time. But there was no way that I could have been prepared for the hysterical screaming and thumping that came from the next room. Although I could not understand what was being shouted at them, it was obvious that the Dutchmen were on the receiving end of a physically violent grilling.

I fearfully waited my turn. Close to panic, I wondered if I would be able to endure the tortuous treatment that I could hear coming from the next room. Just for a moment, my preoccupation with the Dutchmen's ordeal was diverted. One of the Jerry guards put his machine gun down on the desk in front of me. To my amazement, I saw that it was a British Sten gun. The guard was obviously showing out of bravado or maybe, daring someone more stupid than me, to snatch it up and start firing. Armaments such as this, had been dropped by the R.A.F. to the French Maquis and many had been captured by the Germans.

The Dutchmen returned, both badly shaken but still bravely defiant as they suffered further gun-barrel prodding and tongue-lashing from our two guards. Next the German priest was led away. If I thought the Dutchmen had a bad time, it was nothing compared with the severity of the physical and verbal abuse handed out to the priest. The Gestapo were obviously resentful of him being German and of his anti-Hitler, anti-Nazi activities. Considering this, I supposed that from the German point of view, some degree of enmity would be given, but the brutal, malicious and physical attack on the priest answered that thought. I wondered what kind of men these were.

Then it was the R.A.F.'s turn. It was an anticlimax. All we were asked was name, rank and number. There was some suggestion that we were in big trouble because we had been caught in civilian clothes but all had kept our dog tags. It was obvious they knew who we were and where we had come from. The Gestapo searched us, found nothing offensive and sent us back to the ante-room.

The priest and the two Dutchmen were still there, subdued and solemn. The priest was closest to me as we waited for the Hun's next move, "You will go to a prison camp," the Priest whispered. "For me it is death."

I have never forgotten that wretched Man of God nor the words he whispered to me that day in Gestapo headquarters, 80-84 Avenue Foch, Paris, France.

CHAPTER 7

FRESNES - LA PRISON

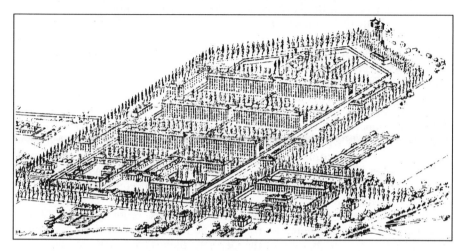

FRESNES PRISON - FROM AN OLD DRAWING.

In silence, we were held for two long hours in that fearful ante-room. Seated bolt upright, even a sideways glance at a companion resulted in a tirade of guttural abuse from one of our captors.

When at last, we were hustled downstairs to another waiting bus, I suppose it was some consolation that the Gestapo had exchanged the prodding barrel of a pilfered Sten gun for a vicious push in the back. We were herded into the back end of the cabin and again driven through the streets of Paris.

Suddenly the two Dutchmen became agitated, alarmed by something they had just heard.

"One of the Germans said we're going to Fresnes," one whispered almost inaudibly. Obviously they were both disturbed and frightened.

I had never heard of Fresnes, but would soon find out all about it. The prison was built in the late 1890s near Fresnes, a small village ten kilometres south of Paris. At that time there were three small overpopulated prisons in the city's centre and it was considered timely to build a new large penitentiary in the country and dispense with the original three.

Fresnes became the largest prison in Europe and was considered to be a model for its time. Each of the three main blocks were four storeys high and contained almost 500 separate cells. Other buildings, such as smaller cell blocks and administrative offices, completed this 45 acre complex.

By the time the Germans occupied the prison in September 1940, Fresnes, the village, had become a suburb of Paris. The first of the three blocks was used by the S.S. and the Wehrmacht (army) for their own purposes. The second block was retained by the French for civil detainees and local criminals who did not interest the Germans. The third block was divided between the S.S. and the Gestapo, the former guarding prisoners condemned by German tribunals and awaiting sentence and the latter holding political and "traitorous" unfortunates who were about to be either shot or transferred to concentration camps in Germany.

"You don't seem afraid, Mijnheer," said one Dutchman almost inaudibly. "You must be very courageous." This reminded me of a similar remark made by Yannick back in Belgium.

My lack of reaction to our situation was due not to bravery but to ignorance. The people of Europe had been under the heel of the Nazis for three years and all had experienced the wrath of the oppressor in one way or another. Some had relatives or friends who had disappeared into institutions like Fresnes, or had witnessed dozens of compatriots shot in retribution for the death of a single German soldier. Others had the experience of their families being broken up and sent to labour and concentration camps in Germany. Of course they feared les Boches. They had cause.

On the other hand, I had no knowledge of the Nazis' brutality and so far had confronted the enemy on equal terms. I had no fear of them - except of death or injury in action maybe, but not of the Germans themselves. After all, was I not British? My ignorance was a blindfold that was soon to be ripped off.

As we approached a pair of large gates in the high south wall, Fresnes looked forbidding indeed. Its reputation, as intimated by the concern of our Dutch comrades, was reinforced by its menacing appearance. Its massive buildings were constructed of dirty brown bricks. Hundreds of small, barred windows in grotesque array, adorned the walls, forecasting what was to come.

Inside the gates we were pushed into one of the smaller buildings and manhandled into separate dog-boxes, each smaller than an average toilet. We had no room to stand and only just enough room to sit on a wooden bench.

That was the last I saw of the old priest and the Dutchmen. I could only guess at what happened to them.

From time to time, the solitude of my lonely kennel was broken by hostile, raucous shouts, often followed by the shriek of some tormented soul in fear or agony. These cries turned my thoughts to my recently farewelled comrades but I was quickly brought back to reality when my dog-box door was pulled open by a green-uniformed soldier about 45 years old.

"Komme mahl raus, schnell." [Come out of there, quickly] he yelled brandishing his Luger menacingly.

Although I did not understand, it was obvious by his antics that I was to come with him. He got no argument from me. He pushed me through a door and out on to the path joining the three large cell blocks. His unerringly-placed Luger found that part of my back already made black and blue by the barrel of the S.D.'s Sten gun.

We entered the easternmost block and I was shoved into a ground level office. Another soldier was sitting behind a desk. I learned later that he was an S.S.

THE FOREBODING WINDOWS OF FRESNES PRISON IN 1990.

feldwebel (sergeant).

"Was ist dien name?" [What is your name] he asked gruffly in Germanic fashion.

"I don't speak German," I said, not understanding him.

"Name?" he said again, louder and impatiently, so I told him my name, rank and number and showed him my dog-tags.

He must have understood, for after I repeated myself a few times he entered the information into a book.

"Wie bist du nach Paris gekommen?" [How did you get to Paris] he asked.

Still not understanding him, I repeated my name, rank and number. He asked a few more questions in German and for his trouble received the same reply. Then, as if he was tired of the whole proceedings, he gave up. I suspect that his job was to do nothing more than 'book me in' and that he was putting on the "Mr. Big" act by assuming the role of an interrogator.

He motioned for me to empty my pockets. The contents, including my now-folded silk map, were put into a calico bag and labelled with Teutonic efficiency.

"Du wirst verhort von der Geheim Poiizie, spater." [You will be interrogated by the Security Police, later] was his parting shot as he motioned for me to be taken away. "Fuhre ihn die zelle zweihundertundzweiundzwanzig." [Put him in cell number two hundred and twenty two] he told my Luger-toting escort.

In a large ablution area, I was ordered to undress and my clothes were taken away. The foul-smelling soap I was obliged to use under the freezing shower that followed, would certainly have been effective had I been bothered by parasitic companions. When they were returned, my clothes stank of fumigating chemicals .

A walking cocktail of evil odours, I was led up a stairway to the first level. I could now see up and down the complete length of the prison. On either side of a huge four-storey central gallery hundreds of closed cell doors converged into the distance.

I was directed up an open flight of stairs to the second level and the perspective of locked doors was even more staggering. As I was shepherded along a narrow walkway, the cells on the other side of the gallery looked like a four-tier stack of huge boxes. A dozen or so S.S. guards opened peep holes at random, ensuring that isolation did not include privacy. One of the peeping Adolfs pushed me roughly aside as he passed by. A few weeks previously I may have retaliated, but not today - Tuesday the 27th July 1943. I was wise enough to know that there is a time and a place for everything and this was certainly not the time nor the place for angry reactions.

Cell number 222 was empty and my Jerry jailer unceremoniously pushed me inside, the steel door slamming shut behind me.

My new pen was a stark cubicle 4 x 2.5 metres x 3 metres high, like most in Fresnes penitentiary. With a door at one end and a window at the other, it too stank of carbolic. The barred, translucent window was 1.5 high x 1 metres wide. The heavy door included a peephole and a port about 10 x 20cm, so that food,

FRESNES PRISON- THE MAIN GALLERY OF EAST BLOCK IN THE PRE-WAR YEARS.

INTERIOR VIEWS OF THE CELLS IN FRESNES PRISON
4 X 2.5 METRES WITH 30 CUBIC METRES OF AIR

etc. could be passed in. To its right was a flagging device for 'service'. In the left corner, a toilet bowl with a water tap over it, reminded me what a long day it had been without such a facility. On one side was a fold-up cot and a wooden table and chair on the other. High above the table was a dim electric light. An aluminium pannikin and spoon, a straw broom, a bucket and a piece of cloth completed the cell's 'gear'.

Everything was painted a clinical light green, now a little the worse for wear. The scratchings on the walls were an historical record of the torment of previous inmates.

During my first half-hour of fearful isolation, I was overcome with self-pity and depression. The day's events, my present loneliness and my doubtful future, brought me to a state of fear and panic. Confined and cut off from human contact, it would have been better if I could have seen out the window or if the door was barred instead of solid.

Helpless and forsaken, for the first time in my life, I was physically and emotionally on my own with no possibility of support or compassion. I sat down on the wooden chair, elbows on the table and put my hands over my eyes in an attempt to obliterate my surroundings. I tried desperately to think of home, of family and friends and of Australia.

I was brought back to reality by the port in the door opening and someone yelling at me in German. I stood quickly and not understanding, stared blankly towards the door. It was flung open and a German soldier stormed into the cell and roughly pulled the fold-up cot down onto its legs.

"Gehen sie schlafen, idioten," [Go to sleep, idiot] he screamed and impatiently pointing to a notice stuck on the wall, said, "lesen sie das." [read that] He then marched out slamming the door behind him. From all this I gathered that it was time for me to get into my cot. I had not noticed in my depressed state that it was now dark outside.

I looked at the notice stuck on the wall but as it was written in French, decided to leave its translation until tomorrow.

I climbed into my cot and pulled the heavy, horse-hair blanket over me. Soon the light was extinguished and lying there in the darkness I became aware of how hungry I was. My last meal had been a light breakfast at the Place d'Italie that morning. It semed so long ago.

My sleep was fitful, interspersed with wondering what quality of fare Fresnes prison was going to offer tomorrow and more to the point, what fate had in store for me.

Next morning, I was rudely awoken by a hammering on the door. I must have reacted in double-quick time because I found myself standing dazed, alongside my cot. Not yet fully awake, I thought it was all part of a ghastly dream that would soon fade away.   It must have been pretty early because light was just beginning to filter through the window and the electric light was on.

Thirty seconds later, I was still trying to gather my senses, when I was brought back to reality by a bad-tempered S.S. guard bursting into my cell. He screamed at me in gibberish, pointing impatiently at my cot. Finally I got the message. He wanted me to make up my blanket and fold the cot up against the wall. Apparently, I did this to his satisfaction for, with a parting, unintelligible remark, he left.

Half an hour later, there was much clanking and clashing outside the door. The light was switched off, the port in the door opened and a different bad-tempered Nazi rattled a food ladle through it. This I understood - breakfast at last. I handed him my pannikin and it came back three-quarters full of coffee. Well, it looked like coffee but it certainly did not taste like coffee. Later, I learned that it was made from acorns but at least the vile-tasting brew was hot. I held my nose and drank the repugnant stuff.

While waiting for the rest of breakfast, my schoolboy French helped to translate most of the notice stuck on the wall.

1:- Get up when the lights go on in the morning.
2:- Make bed and clean cell.
3:- Coffee follows when light goes off.
4:- Soup midday.
5:- Go to bed when light goes on in the evening.
There were a few other instructions but that was the gist of it.

Then it dawned on me that breakfast was just the coffee and that I must wait until midday to eat again. I was already very hungry and the coffee had not helped.

I used the toilet and turned on the tap above it to flush. As this did not work, I was nonplussed and decided to call for assistance. I gamely flagged for 'service' and waited.

Five minutes later a guard came in. I mimed pulling a non-existent chain over the toilet. He understood my problem immediately, and filling the bucket with water, threw the lot into the toilet, successfully flushing it. He looked at me with burlesque pity, circling his fore-finger around his temple and obviously wondering where I had been all my life.

"Dummer Englander," [Dumb Englishman] he said as he left my cell laughing his head off. And I thought the Master Race had no sense of humour. Maybe just toilet humour!

Sitting at my table I decided that I must keep active and fit. If I lapsed into mindless oblivion, then I would succumb to my adversity and be much worse off. I therefore resolved to exercise regularly, first by pacing my cell, four metres - four paces back and forth - one hundred times - eight hundred paces - perhaps over half a mile. Trying it out, I found that it had the added advantage of passing the time more quickly but unfortunately, added to my hunger.

At long last I heard the food trolley stop outside my door. My midday meal had arrived and by this time, the pangs of hunger were almost unbearable. In a high state of expectancy, I passed out my pannikin. It was returned full of a yellowish-brown liquid with bits of potatoes and turnips floating in it. Then I was disgusted to see it was infested with vermin. As hungry as I was, I could not face that nauseating mess and in tears, threw the repulsion down the toilet.

The afternoon that followed was the most miserable I had ever spent in my life. Hardly out of my teens, I certainly had grown up over the last month or so. Now hungry, frightened and alone, it seemed I was about to grow up some more.

At long last the light came on, signalling that I must get into my cot. As I tried desperately for oblivion, I fantasised of home but the gnawing in my belly made sleep impossible. After two or three hours, I got up and paced up and down only to be screamed at by one of the peeping Adolphs.

The following morning it was "coffee" again. Then at midday, one thin slice of sour black bread accompanied the same revolting soup. This time I devoured the lot. It had only taken two days for me to learn that when you are hungry enough, you will eat anything.

Two more lonely days later, I found out that it was possible to talk to a nearby inmate through a vent just above my cot. My contact was French so our conversations were pretty hopeless. Nevertheless, I did find out that he was a communist Jew, meaning that his chance of survival was a lot slimmer than mine. This diversion was cut short one day by a Hun guard bursting into my cell. "Halt dinen mund, Englischer schweinhund." [Shut your mouth, English pig dog] he said as he took a swipe at me.

"Alle Englischer schweinhund." [All Englishmen are pig dogs] he went on.

Well, that was too much. Twice now I had been described in this manner. I understood "Englischer" and I thought that "schweinhund" meant "bastard" and it was time that I put things right. In English I said, "I'm not an English bastard, I'm an Australian bastard." Although I knew he had not understood me, I gained some personal satisfaction by being a loyal Aussie, even under such adverse circumstances.

Ten more hungry, solitary days passed before I was taken out for exercise. By this time I was weak and tottery through lack of food and exertion of any kind seemed to be ridiculous.

A dozen exercise yards ran along either side of the main building, each

THE EXERCISE YARDS IN FRESNES PRISON

measuring about four by eight metres. Iron bars at both ends and a three-metre high wall on each side completed the enclosure.

"Bewege dich! Laufe rum." [Move yourself! Run around] the guard said, making a circling motion with his arm. I guessed that I was expected to take a walk around the compound. I kept it up as long as I could, but dizzy, I sat down on a corner bench. After about a quarter of an hour, I was taken back to my cell, much the worse for wear, I feared.

For ten fearful days, I tried various ways to help myself endure the uncertainty and the endless boredom of my loathsome cell. My half-mile walk twice daily up and down, was still something of a diversion. Time also passed as I picked the dead creepy-crawlies out of my soup each day. Many hours were spent designing houses, using pieces of straw from the broom. I laid them meticulously end to end on my tabletop, perhaps an attempt to become absorbed in something, anything, prompted an architecture degree after the war. Unfortunately, after all that had happened, like many ex-servicemen, I was unable to settle down and study.

I was now feeling dizzy each time I exercised or stood up too quickly. Constantly and painfully hungry, I was losing weight fast. I thought of the emaciated condition of some of my fellow inmates after spending years in this diabolical prison. Was this to be my fate as well?

Then came the day when I learned just a little of what went on in this wretched prison in 1943. It was about nine o'clock in the morning, when my cell door opened and a guard motioned for me to follow him, screaming out the now familiar. "Schnell, schnell." [Quickly, quickly]

I was taken to a room on the ground floor and stood in front of a table behind which two men were seated, one in civilian clothes, the other in a German S.S. officer's uniform. The civilian immediately started yelling at me in German. He was extremely agitated and the tirade went on for about a minute.

"This is Kommissar Gansler from the Gestapo," the S.S. officer eventually said in perfect English. "He is the interrogating officer. I am Hauptmann Handke of the S.S.. I will interpret.

"Kommissar Gansler has charged you with being a spy. What do you say to that?" His bellow was quiet, for a German that is.

I stated my name, rank and number, producing another tirade from the Gestapo man.

"He says that if you aren't more co-operative you'll be shot as a spy. After all, you were captured in civilian clothes."

I repeated my name, rank and number.

"How did you get to Paris?" Hauptmann Handke asked. "Also, we want the names of the people who helped you in Belgium."

Now that was a slip, as I had not mentioned Belgium at any time to anyone. They obviously knew more about my movements than they let on.

Again I quoted my name, rank and number and added, "I wish to see a representative of the Red Cross." More fanatical jabbering from the excited Kommissar and this time he shook his fist in my face.

"Because you'll not help us and because you're in civilian clothes, you'll be taken out and shot as an English spy," the Hauptmann translated.

I showed them my dog tags. "That proves that I'm in the Royal Australian Air Force and that I'm protected by the Geneva Convention, just as all German Luftwaffe officers are who have been taken prisoners in England."

Again Kommissar Gansler took over in bellowing German, but I suspected that he understood more English than he was willing to admit.

I had now been on my feet for about twenty minutes and was very sick and very dizzy but I gritted my teeth. There was no way that these two Jerries were going to have the satisfaction of seeing me keel over.

"We don't know if your identity tags are genuine," said Handke. "As far as we're concerned you're an English spy and we know how to deal with English spies."

"What sort of a spy would I make?" I blurted out. I was scared and my voice was unsteady as I went on. "I'm Australian, not English. I don't know anything about France or Europe and I don't speak French or German. Surely they'd choose someone more competent than me."

"Who helped you in Belgium?" asked Hauptmann Handke again.

"You wouldn't be very proud of a German soldier who answered that question for an English interrogator, would you?" I countered.

It was obvious that the Gestapo man was losing interest and after another spell of abuse, he motioned for me to be taken away.

"The charge that you're an English spy still stands," was Hauptmann Handke's parting remark, "We'll now consider what to do with you," he added.

Back in my cell, I felt nauseous and drained. I was satisfied with the outcome but I had been shaken by their threats. Surely they realised that I was nothing more than an evading airman. I would have been very much more terrified had I known then what I learned some years later; the fearful menace of Fresnes and the bestial activities of the Gestapo at the prison.

One such victim was Odette Marie Celine Brailly. Born in April 1912, she grew up in Amiens and later in Boulogne. At nineteen she married Roy Sanson, an Englishman and in 1933 they moved to England with their daughter. Two more girls were born soon after.

Odette was grief stricken when France fell to the Nazis in 1940 and at times she felt a little ashamed of the comparatively safe life she lived whilst her French sisters were suffering the privations of occupied France.

Even though she was distressed at having to leave her children in the care of friends, in 1942 Odette joined the French section of the Special Operations Executive. Her intimate knowledge of France and the French people and her fluency in the language, was considered invaluable. After strenuous training in self defence, morse code, parachuting, German uniform recognition and other skills, in August 1942 she was sent to France by way of Gibraltar, with the code name of "Lise".

There she met and worked with Captain Peter Churchill, alias Monsieur Pierre Chauvert, code name "Raoul". Odette gained the reputation of being a courageous, clever and diligent agent. She undertook many dangerous tasks usually assigned to experienced males. The three, Raoul, Arnaud (radio

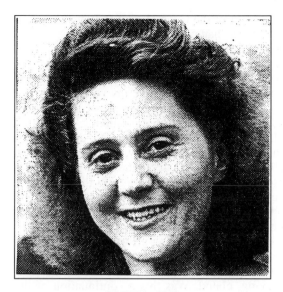

ODETTE – 1949.

operator) and Lise formed a formidable team of hindrance to the German occupying forces.

With Raoul, she was captured by the Abwehr [Counter Intelligence Service] in April 1943 at Annecy, in eastern France. Eventually she and Peter Churchill were handed over to the Gestapo and imprisoned in Fresnes on the 8th May 1943.

Even though she was starved and humiliated by the S.S. women guards, she never lost her natural dignity. She was interrogated more than ten times by the Gestapo and at no time did she divulge the information they so cruelly sought. On one occasion the sadistic Gestapo interviewer introduced a red hot iron to her back and on another, she underwent the traumatic agony of having her toe nails withdrawn on both feet. It is hard for 'ordinary' people to understand the obscenities that Hitler's butchers happily inflicted on their fellow human beings.

Odette claimed the name Churchill, hoping that it would help her with the Gestapo. Nevertheless, she was condemned to death but survived an horrific two-month journey to the infamous women's concentration camp at Ravensbruck, 75 Kilometres north of Berlin.

No less than 100,000 women perished at Ravensbruck during the war. Even this perversion fades into insignificance when compared with the 2,000,000 men, women and children incinerated at Auschwitz.

Odette spent many months in solitary confinement and complete darkness where she suffered bashings, intense hunger pains, dysentery and scurvy. Finally, in 1945, her use of the surname Churchill helped her. The Kommandant of Ravensbruck drove her to the American lines in the hope that he would be credited with ensuring her survival. With his score of 100,000 dead women it was not to be. In 1946 King George V1 awarded Odette Sanson the George Cross for extraordinary courage in the face of the enemy. Never was an award more richly deserved.

There were hundreds of others who, like Odette and Peter Churchill were fellow inmates of mine in Fresnes. To name a few: Madame Renee Haultecoeur was imprisoned in July 1943 and sent to Ravensbruck in January 1944. Madame Yvonne de la Rochefoucauld, British agent, tortured, sent to Ravensbruck, November 1943.

Madame Geneviere de Gaulle, a sister of the General, sent to Ravensbruck in 1943. General Delestraint, executed at Dachau concentration camp.

Mademoiselle Francine Fromond, 22 years old, shot in Fresnes prison.

It was just as well for my own sanity, that I did not know of those atrocities as I walked unsteadily out of that Gestapo interrogation room.

About a week later, just after the 'plat du jour' arrived, my cell door opened and a guard motioned for me to follow him. With the threats of my Gestapo interrogators still haunting me, frightened I hesitated. Glancing around the comparative sanctuary of my cell, I wondered if I would ever see it again.

"Herauskommen schnell, schnell." [Come out quickly, quickly] the guard yelled. Expecting the worst, I followed him downstairs to the office where I was originally 'booked in' to the prison. The S.S. feldwebel was still there. He took all my meagre possessions, except for my silk map, out of the calico bag and gave them to me. Then, I was locked in an adjoining room.

My fears subsided somewhat because I argued that if Jerry intended to do me a mischief, it was unlikely that he would bother giving me back my belongings. Half an hour later I was still worrying about my captor's next move when suddenly the door opened and my navigator, Clarrie Craven, stumbled in.

"Clarrie," I screamed, unbelieving, elated. Was this a continuation of the crazy dream that started two months before with exploding flak shells over Wuppertal?

"Skipper," Clarrie shouted incredulously, "I thought you were dead. I did, I thought you were dead."

"Bloody hungry but certainly not dead," I laughed, slapping him on the back. I told Clarrie how I had jumped from our Lancaster soon after he had.

"You must have been bloody fast," he said. "It exploded as I was floating down."

"Fast isn't the word," I answered. "The bit about the Captain going down with the ship didn't grab me, you can believe it."

We were both jabbering away, each trying to tell his own story and getting nowhere, when the door burst open again and my bomb aimer, Norm Conklin, was pushed roughly into the room.

"Clarrie," he yelled. Then he saw me. "Skipper, I thought you'd been killed."

"We've been through that already, Normie" I said, delighted at seeing him. "Who next, I wonder?"

"Well, Dennis is here somewhere," said Clarrie. "He was caught with me."

"And what about Rowdy, Frank and Col. What happened to them?"

"I don't know," Clarrie replied, "but I'm sure we all got out of the aircraft."

"Thank God for that. It's rare for all the crew to survive. We're very lucky."

"Does anyone know the date?" Norm asked.

"Yes, it's the 24th of August, 1943," Clarrie answered.

Our happy reunion was cut short by the S.S. feldwebel. He had two other soldiers with him and I noticed that their uniforms were a blue-grey colour.

"You go to Germany," he said in poor English. "These two Luftwaffe guards will escort you."

Outside Fresnes at last, we were bundled into the back of a military truck, with our two Luftwaffe guards.

"No talk," one ordered. His manner was a little less authoritative than we had been used to from the Master Race, over the last month or so. Even though hunger still gnawed painfully away, tension abated to some extent. Now we were away from the menace of Fresnes, the Gestapo and the S.S. Now we had Luftwaffe guards.

Trucked back through Paris once again, we crossed the Pont St. Michel, catching a glimpse of the Notre-Dame Cathedral and in the gathering dusk, we arrived at the Gare de l'Est.

Herded into a regular compartment of a passenger train, we were seated with our two guards opposite us. Other travellers tried to claim empty seats but were ordered away.

A shrill whistle and a gush of steam, and we took our leave of the unhappy memories of sorrowful Paris. We were on our way to Nazi Germany and an uncertain future.

Even so, we had left behind a record to be envied. One night out on the town in Paris, followed by a month in the slammer, was a performance that deserved the admiration of all dedicated revellers. Proudly this had been accomplished by the crew of Lancaster D-Donald. Well, by some of us anyway!

At about 10pm, one of the guards took a loaf of bread and a monster strasbourg sausage from his kit bag. The three of us had been trying to doze but suddenly, in a flash, we were wide awake. Nearly driven mad by the aroma of the sausage and salivating profusely, we pathetically waited for our German friend to cut off our share.

We waited and waited and waited. Crazy with hunger, we watched every bite, every mouthful, every swallow. To famished souls like us, this simple fare was an orgy of mastication, a gluttony of over-indulgence. When not even a crumb was left to ease our torment, we just closed our eyes and tried not to hate the Jerry jerk and his sadistic lack of understanding.

Whatever our destination, it was going to be a slow journey as It took 14 hours to travel the first 400 kilometres from Paris to Saarbrucken.

During that night, hunger and the continual motion of the train's stopping and restarting, made sleep impossible. I used the time to tell Clarrie and Norm, amongst other things, of my cell at Fresnes and the Gestapo questioning. They were surprised, for both had shared a cell with French prisoners and neither had been interrogated.

We reached our destination at four o'clock in the afternoon now desperately hungry and thirsty as our last meal had been the Fresnes's excuse for soup, twenty-eighty hours before. As the train pulled slowly into a platform, busy with late-afternoon commuters, I saw on the station sign-board the name Frankfurt-am-Main.

THE LOCATION OF EUROPEAN POW CAMPS.

(COURTESY: AWM)

CHAPTER 8

DULAG LUFT

ONE ASPECT OF DULAG LUFT IN 1943

As soon as we got off the Paris - Frankfurt train, our guards pushed us towards the exit gates. We nervously threaded our way through jostling German citizenry, who looked intent on getting home before the whine of air-raid sirens drove them wearily into their shelters.

Then, one of our guards stupidly announced to all and sundry that we were "Englischer terrorfliegers." [English terror fliers] The word spread like wild-fire. Before long Clarrie, Norm and I were surrounded by a crowd of screaming, irate men and women hitting and spitting at us. Their bitter resentment was understandable after the carnage caused by the relentless annihilation of Hamburg a month before. Continuous bomber raids by the R.A.F. at night and the U.S.A.A.F. by day, had raised the city.

Seeing raw hate in the Germans' eyes, was terrifying and would no doubt have been the same if they had been Londoners and we were Luftwaffe crew. As far as Frankfurters were concerned, we were merciless murderers; the tyrants from above; the ones to blame for the loss of loved ones and all the suffering inflicted on the German people.

Our justification was, that we were part of an Armada of heroes liberating Europe from under the heel of the ruthless Nazi boot. It seems that it all depended which side you were on. Naturally the aggrieved citizens of Frankfurt saw it only from their point of view. No doubt, we were saved from serious injury because we wore civilian clothes.

The melee became so confused that the angry citizens began venting their spleen on all and sundry, unsure of who was friend and who was foe. Our guards roughly but quickly pushed us through the exit gate, towards what turned out to be a suburban railway station. We boarded a commuter train for Oberursel, a town about ten miles to the north-west of Frankfurt and a compartment was cleared for us, to ensure that there would not be a repeat of the shemozzle at Frankfurt station.

Travelling through the suburbs, it was intriguing to see familiar names on factories, General Motors of the U.S.A. for example. This American plant was manufacturing munitions for use against the Allies, as were German-owned plants in Britain and America; producing war materials to be used against the Axis. It was a strange world indeed.

We left the train at Oberursel station and boarded a tramcar which took us through town and then to the Kupforhammer stop, about two miles away - our destination, the close by Luftwaffe Interrogation Centre; Dulag-Luft. This area had originally been an agricultural school and was taken over by the Luftwaffe in 1939. It became Durchgangslage Luft [Air Transit Camp], abbreviated to Dulag Luft. From then on, all British and American airmen were taken there for interrogation.

It included the Interrogation Centre, a P.O.W. Transit Camp and a hospital in nearby Hohemark. Later, on September 10th 1943, the Transit Camp was moved to Palmengarten [Palm Garden] only a kilometre or so from the main railway station in the centre of Frankfurt. This was a target area and contrary to Geneva Convention.

Following persistent objections by the British and American Governments, through the Red Cross, Dulag Luft transit camp was finally re-established at Wetzlar, 50 Kilometres north of Frankfurt-am-Main.

Clarrie, Norm and I arrived at Dulag Luft late on the 24th August 1943, too exhausted, too desperately hungry and too utterly depressed to worry about such matters. By then, the three of us had been half-starved for over a month. Moreover, we had not eaten at all for thirty hours since leaving Fresnes. We could hardly stand, let alone walk. It was only about a hundred yards from the tramway to the barbed-wire gates of Dulag Luft but even that short distance exhausted us.

An eight-foot barbed wire fence surrounded a long, single-storey U shaped wooden building. Barred windows close together foretold the purpose of the tiny rooms inside.

We were directed to the only two-storey building in the compound, immediately to the right of the entrance gates. The guards pushed us unceremoniously into a small ground floor room, slamming the door shut behind us.

"This is bloody inhuman," Norm said. "When do we get something to eat?"

"They'll have to move us before nightfall," Clarrie observed. "There's nowhere to sleep in here. Maybe they'll feed us then."

I looked around the room. He was right. There was nowhere to lay down or for that matter, nowhere to sit, except on the stone floor. Just then the door opened and a Luftwaffe guard came in.

"Stooke," he said gruffly.

"Yes," I replied apprehensively.

"Come with me," he ordered, "you others wait." His English was perfect. and he led me up the stairs on the outside of the building and into an office.

An Oberleutnant sat behind a desk looking at some papers. I swayed in front of him for at least a minute before he looked up.

"I have your name, rank and number. Repeat them to me," he ordered and that I did.

"Correct. Now your date of birth." I repeated my name, rank and number but this time added "Sir", in military fashion.

"Now don't be stupid," he said impatiently. "I need your date of birth, birthplace, religion, civil occupation, nationality, father's name and address, married status, children, mother's maiden name for identity purposes. We won't be able to tell your next of kin that you're safe unless you tell us these things."

This seemed reasonable but one question leads to another and before long I might be spilling the beans - not that I had any beans to spill.

"We have most of this information, anyway," he went on. "Now what's your date of birth?"

Again I replied with my name, rank, and number accompanied by "Sir", but he lost his temper, "You're a bloody fool and an idiot." he yelled. "We'll get it out of you anyway." He turned to the guard standing alongside me. "Take this dummkopf away."

I was trundled into another room where my tonette and faulty watch were taken from me and put into a bag. I was photographed, fingerprinted, measured, weighed and injected with who-knows-what, stripped of my civilian clothes and showered. My shoes and socks were returned, along with a blue neck-to-knee undergarment worn by American aircrew to keep out the cold.

Outside again, I was taken to the long U shaped building called the "cooler". It was made up of over 120 cells on either side of a main corridor. I was put into number 52, a 5 foot x 12 foot box which included a cot, a table, a chair and a bell to call the guard. A pannikin on the table reminded me of my hunger and raised my hopes. I waited for a minute or so to bolster my courage, then rang the bell. After about five minutes the door opened.

"What do you want, terrorflieger," the guard said peevishly. Maybe I had caught him just as he was about to go on leave to Oberursel.

"Food and water," I said, showing just a little aggression. "I have been starved in prison for 30 days and have not eaten for 30 hours. Neither have my two companions who arrived with me."

"Night rations are finished." He marched out of my cell angrily, mumbling to himself. A short time later, another guard brought me two slices of black bread and a cup of water.

"Thank you," I said. Believe me, I really meant it. I nibbled that sour, black revolting bread in an almost ritualistic fashion, trying desperately to make it last as long as possible. Revolting? Not so!! The bread tasted like cake and the water like wine.

Later, Clarrie and Norm told me they were also given a ration of bread that

THE CELLS AT DULAG LUFT IN 1943

night. I like to think that I initiated it.

As I tried to sleep through the onset of dysentery, I fantasised uproarious orgies where the main attraction was not a shapely wench bursting out of a monstrous cake but the cake itself. Believe me, hunger can be much more effective than a cold shower to quench your libido.

Early next morning I was awoken by guards handing out another two slices of bread and a cup of ersatz coffee. Again, I ate reverently and slowly, savouring every bite.

Whenever nature called, a guard had to accompany the prisoner to an open toilet at the end of the main corridor. There were quite a few of us with mild and some with acute dysentery, consequently the guards were kept pretty busy. I wondered what their answer might be, should a proud offspring ask his uniformed 'Vater' [father], "What did you do during the war, Papa?"

Midway through the morning, a little man in civilian clothes entered my cell, claiming that he was from the German Red Cross. Again his English was perfect - it seems that everyone spoke perfect English at Dulag Luft.

"I notice on your P.O.W. card that there are a number of questions yet unanswered," he said. "Now be reasonable. Unless we identify you properly, we don't know that you're not a spy. The Gestapo shoots spies and I can't protect you from them. Also we want to get in touch with your parents to tell them you're safe. Now be a good chap and answer these questions."

I had been thinking about this dilemma. If the questions were those the Oberleutnant had asked me last night, surely there would be no harm in answering them. I told him my birth date, place of birth, religion, nationality, father's name and address, mother's maiden name, marital status, etc.

"Thank you," he said amicably. "Now just a couple more questions and I'll be finished. What was your squadron and where's..."

I cut him off in mid-sentence. "I won't answer that," I said. "That information isn't the business of the Red Cross and by having asked such questions, I'm led to believe that you're not from that organisation."

"Don't get smart with me," he yelled in Germanic fashion. All pleasantness had gone. "You can rot in this cell for all I care."

As he stomped out angrily, I thought what a peculiar Red Cross Man he was.

Soon after he left, the mid-day soup arrived. It was no better than the offering at Fresnes, except the pannikin was a bit bigger and it contained no creepy-crawlies. It was just as watery and no more satisfying.

That afternoon I took a close look at the cell window which had been painted over from the outside. Squinting out through a scratch in one of the panels I could see a field, then a barbed-wire fence and beyond, on a slight rise, a group of typical German houses. Most were two-storey, their high gabled roofs testifying that in winter it snowed heavily in Oberursel.

To relieve the boredom, I asked a guard if I could open the window for a while. "Nein, es verboten." [No] was his curt reply, [it's forbidden]

That evening, two more slices of black bread with a small ration of pumpkin jam was issued, along with the usual ersatz coffee. Daily rations at Dulag Luft were confirmed as four slices of bread, sometimes with pumpkin jam, two cups of acorn coffee and one bowl of watery soup. No chance of getting fat on that lot.

Later I learnt that in 1943 one thousand British and American airmen passed through Dulag Luft each month. By mid-1944 this figure grew to three thousand and at times, my small cell held five prisoners.

Thankfully the dysentery from the night before abated. Although wakened from time to time by air raid sirens, I slept a little better during my second night at Dulag Luft.

Next morning, just after 'breakfast', I received a visit from a smartly-dressed Luftwaffe Offizier. If I thought that everyone at Dulag Luft spoke English fluently, I had not heard anything yet. This man must have been an Oxford Blue for sure and later flown Spitfires in the R.A.F!

"Hello old boy, my name is Kurt Schmidt. Have a Players [cigarette]. Bad show to see you in these scruffy billets but things are bound to improve. You pranged two months ago so you must have been on the run for some time. Good show. Now I have to go through this bloody boring questioning bit, so let's get it over with then we can have a natter about Australia and more particularly Melbourne. I've walked down Collins Street, you know."

I sat back astounded. I might as well have been talking to a toffy Wing Commander back in England. I was surprised to find that the Players cigarette had somehow found its way into my hand and was already alight.

"I have a card here for you to fill in whenever you wish. Then we can inform your pater that you are fit as a trout." He put the card down on the table.

"Sorry to tell you, old chap, but as you have been off the squadron for a while you wouldn't know that Flight Sergeant Fuhrmann finally bought it over

Hamburg last month. And just after he got his D.F.M. too. Rotten luck after all he had been through."

Now I was flabbergasted. Fuhrmann had done about fifteen operations and his aircraft had been badly damaged on almost every raid. I did not say a word, and yet my open-mouthed astonishment must have confirmed that I was from 460 Squadron and that I knew F/Sgt Fuhrmann.

"We found your Lanc', of course, near Alken in Belgium. Here is a photo." He showed me a photograph of a part of the fuselage with a big 'D' on it. "You must have been hit by flak over Wuppertal, eh?"

I had been with the Luftwaffe officer for over five minutes and this was the first direct question he had asked. He had been so hail-fellow-well-met, so fraternally R.A.F., that I could have easily answered him off the cuff, just as I would an aircrew mate back at the squadron.

To tell him that D-Donald had been shot down by flak did not seem important in itself. Nevertheless it would have confirmed the effectiveness of their anti-aircraft barrages and searchlight batteries. Also, the downing of D-Donald could not be claimed as a 'kill' by some Nazi night fighter pilot. More importantly, a reply would have led to even more pointed questioning. Unimportant queries are raised by clever interrogators to test an airman's readiness to talk too much.

"I can't answer that, sir," I replied.

"No matter," he laughed. "Anyway we know from the damage to your kite that it was flak. That's right, isn't it?" I remained silent.

He asked about the Lancaster. What it was like to fly. What were its take-off and landing characteristics, its cruising speeds, etc. His questions were cleverly buried in his own observations, like, "The Packard Merlin certainly increased the Lancs' climb rate, didn't it?"

As I did not answer him, he took out a typed copy of 'Pilot's Notes for the Lancaster' from his briefcase. Where had he got that from? Some idiot must have had a copy aboard when he pranged. What a clot! Maybe I was the clot! Obviously he knew as much about the Lanc' as I did. Possibly more.

Finally I said to him, "Look sir, how can I compete verbally with you. I'm just run-of-the-mill aircrew. You're a clever, highly-trained interrogator." You never know, flattery might have got me everywhere! "If I say anything at all," I went on, "you'll soon have me talking my head off. So I'll remain silent. When it comes to the point, what could I tell you anyway?"

"Oh well, Stooke," he said, "we'll hold you here for a while longer. I'll have another chat with you in a couple of days."

"Could I have the window open for a while?" I asked him.

"I'll see what I can do," he promised.

Later, I found out how interrogation methods had changed over the previous year or so. Earlier prisoners had been confined in unbearably overheated cells, threatened with violence and even death as spies, unless questions were answered. They were abused and called "murderers of children" and "terror fliers". Concocted shootings of fellow crewmen was another device often used. Apparently these tactics were not as successful as the friendly approach I experienced.

During the morning a guard came and told me that I was permitted to open the window of the cell. I had forgotten how pleasant it was to sit quietly and gaze out into the countryside, albeit German. The intervening barbed-wire fence spoilt the scenery to some extent but after several weeks staring at confining blank walls, the rolling countryside around Oberursel was most acceptable.

A man approached my window, his clothes bedraggled and with wooden clogs on his feet. Apparently his job was to clean up the area, weeding and picking up papers, etc.

He spoke in a language I had never heard before, gesticulating in an attempt to aid understanding. He plunged a dirty finger into his chest and said proudly, "Russki, Russki." I had met my first of many Russian prisoners-of-war.

Contrary to the promise made by Herr Schmidt to revisit me, the next morning I was moved to one of two transit huts, a hundred yards or so from the cells. A corridor separated rooms to right and left, each designed to hold twelve men. Still in my comical American blue 'long johns', I was unceremoniously pushed into a room that already held at least thirty British and American airmen.

Where were Clarrie and Norm? I looked around in vain. After a month of having Jerry breathing down my neck, I was keen to have a comparatively unfettered confab with someone, anyone. Then I noticed how shocked and tired these men looked. Some were wounded and had not yet been attended to.

I tried to imagine the state of mind of the American airmen, who only two or three days ago, had stepped confidently into their Flying Fortresses with typical youthful bravado. In formation, they had crossed the Dutch coast in broad daylight and from that moment on, had been constantly attacked by hundreds of Nazi fighters in the air, and anti-aircraft batteries on the ground. Maybe they had seen a B-17 from their squadron explode, scattering the aircraft and their buddies high and wide. And maybe, as another bomber, on fire, spun towards earth, they prayed that they might see all 10 parachutes blossom before the aircraft crashed. Some had buddies killed alongside them but even if severely wounded and in pain, these brave men would have continued to do their job. Then suddenly their turn had come. With shells from a FW-190 shattering wings and fuselage, the order would have been given to "Abandon Aircraft." With the earth 20,000 feet below, they had jumped into nothingness. Without oxygen and fighting for breath, they would have felt the jerk of their parachute, leaving no time to be concerned whether it would open or not. As distressed as they were, they would still have looked around anxiously for the white canopies of comrades. As they neared the ground, it would have rushed up frighteningly to meet them. If they were lucky they would have missed the many bone-crushing hazards that awaited them. But some would have fallen into fires of their own making and been incinerated.

Confused, hurt and frightened, those that survived had yet to face the wrath of the German people and for many, that was a final humiliation. It was the 'lucky' ones who ended up at Dulag Luft and after interrogation, were in this room. Now the first pangs of hunger could be added to their misery and uncertainty. How their situation had changed in a few short days.

A U.S.A.A.F. lieutenant, wearing the wings of a pilot, was standing near the window. We had something in common to talk about so I introduced myself. His reaction at first surprised me as he drew back in mistrust and was completely unresponsive to my approach.

Then I understood. If I had been accosted under the same circumstances by a stranger dressed in ridiculous blue long johns, I would have been just as suspicious. Quite rightly he believed me to be a German spy, placed amongst Allied airmen to gain unbridled information. I backed away, speculating on my chances of being done away with that night by chauvinists detailed to do the job.

Thankfully, before that could happen, a guard called my name and I was taken to a clothing store at the end of the corridor. My tonette and faulty watch were returned and I was issued with underclothes, a shirt, a pair of British army battledress trousers and an American army G.I. tunic. At least I looked something like an allied soldier - a variegated one.

Hustled back into the same room as before, I seemed to be better accepted, even by the Yank lieutenant. Not that we had time to fraternise because in the afternoon, the Americans were taken away and did not come back. I guessed that they were on their way to a permanent camp. At least I was able to find a bunk for the night.

And so it was that on Wednesday, 1st September, 1943 the R.A.F. prisoners were paraded in front of Oberstleutnant Otto Becker, Camp Kommandant, Dulag Luft. I was relieved to see that Clarrie and Norm were in this group. They must have been in one of the other rooms. I quickly moved in beside them.

Oberst' Becker told us in English that we were to go by train to our permanent camp in Saxony. "For you the war is over," he told us, "you would be very foolish to try to escape on the way as the guards have orders to shoot." He said that we would be issued with 'plenty' of food for the journey, just like the trip from Fresnes, I thought, and then he wished us good fortune for the future. Except for the bit about shooting, an observer might have thought that we were going on a group holiday to a fabulous Black Forest resort.

He was right about the issue of food with each of us receiving a small bit of sausage, a quarter loaf of black bread and two cans of Red Cross [English] stew. This seemed generous for a short train journey to Saxony, only 300 miles away.

As ordered, we formed up in columns of five and to be sure that all were present, the Feldwebel in charge marched along the ranks counting in fives. As this procedure became a never-ending monotony, repeated daily, throughout a prisoner-of-war's captivity, the German words funf, zehn, funfzehn, zwanzig, funfundzwanzig, etc. [five, ten, fifteen, twenty, twenty-five, etc.] will live in memory forever.

The Feldwebel saluted Oberst' Becker and reported a full complement of 'Kriegys'. There were 147 of us in the group and without delay, we were marched away from Dulag Luft, led by the Feldwebel, with twenty armed Luftwaffe guards spread along both sides of our column.

We turned left into Hoemarkstrasse with a march of two and a half miles to Oberursel railway station. Our pace was slow, as some were wounded and others were suffering from dysentery.

Waiting for us in the Oberursel goods yard was our transport, two ancient, dirty cattle trucks plundered from France, possibly during World War One, each labelled, "6 chevaux ou 40 hommes." [6 horses or 40 men.]

"Surely they're not going to cram us into those filthy trucks?" Norm exclaimed in horror.

"There are only two, anyway," mathematician Clarrie began to calculate, "147 men, 40 men per truck. We need at least a couple more. I wonder when they'll get here."

The Feldwebel counted us again in fives; "Funf, zehn, funfzehn, etc.," then divided us into two groups. "Get in, get in. Quickly, schnell, schnell," the guards yelled. First there was disbelief, then anger, when it was realised that over seventy men were to be jammed into a space originally considered just adequate for 40.

Some began to climb in, helping the wounded and sick. Others hung back until they saw rifle butts being used on those who refused. Inevitably our captors won the day and with everyone inside, the doors were slammed shut.

Clarrie, Norm and I managed to stay together and together we certainly were. There was hardly enough room to stand, let alone sit. Lying down on the straw-covered floor was out of the question. There was much pushing and shoving until one man, I never found out his name, made himself heard, "We're all in this together and we're all going to survive," he shouted. "Fighting amongst ourselves is not on. Now listen to me."

He organised us into 12 groups of five or six - Group A and B worked together, as did C and D and so on. In this way some were able to sit or even lie down whilst others stood. From time to time everybody swapped over.

After about three hours, the trucks had not moved and with no air flow, the atmosphere became very foul. As quietly as possible, we removed boards from the sides of the trucks, hoping to increase the ventilation but our vandalism did not help much.

Relieving ourselves became a major problem and some began to use the gaps in the sides of the truck. Seeing this, the German guards hit at the urinaters with their rifle butts, calling out in German, "filthy English bastards." Apparently they expected us to piddle into the straw.

What of the other bodily function? After much straining and levering, a loose floor board was removed in one corner and this became the toilet for 70 men. To reach it meant tramping over and mostly on, your mates. Finally, when you got there, you found yourself in a queue. This was rough on the dysentery sufferers as they had to wait in pain with legs crossed.

Just after dark, we heard the hiss and puff of a steam engine and with a rowdy crash, our trucks recoiled as we were joined to the engine. Then with a torturous jerk and a violent rebound, we slowly gathered speed - at last we were on our way to Saxony, 300 miles away.

The train ground to a jarring halt at least a dozen times during the next two hours. Each stop triggered off a deafening metal-to-metal staccato of sound as couplings slammed together. This hammering was accompanied by violent lurchings back-and-forth, throwing 70 tightly-packed men savagely against the sides of the cattle truck and each other. This jarring and lurching was repeated each time the train moved off again. With the train under way, violent side-to-side and back-and-forth pitching, plus clicking wheels, rattles and vibrations all contributed to the turmoil within. We were smothered by movement and noise. Some relief was found by those whose turn it was to sit down.

A longer stop than usual with much hissing and puffing, resulted in our being uncoupled from the engine and parked in the railway yards at Frankfurt-am-Main. We had only travelled a seemingly endless ten miles from Oberursel.

The rest of the night and all through the next day, we were left packed together in those motionless, putrid cattle trucks. Fearful, we heard air raid sirens warning the Germans and us, of an impending bombing attack by the R.A.F or the U.S.A.A.F. Our fears were unfounded but the people of Berlin were not so lucky.

The everlasting day dragged on. Clarrie, Norm and I carefully rationed the food as we had been on short rations for a long time and knew well of the pain brought on by days of hunger. We tried to warn others that, judging by our progress so far, it would take longer than at first thought to travel the 300 miles to Saxony. They would have been well advised to apportion their food carefully but not many took our advice.

By dusk the stench and heat were unbelievable. Even those who were not suffering with dysentery were exhausted and dehydrated. Two buckets of water had been passed to us but had not lasted long. Mercifully, at long last, we were hitched onto another engine and were on our way again, grateful to be breathing fresh air. Once again, we had to suffer the horrors of that noisy, bucking cattle truck in motion. Six hours later at dawn, we were unhitched in the railway yards of Gottingen, exhausted.

During that day, we were allowed out of our hell on wheels for two periods of half an hour. There was a water tank nearby and a hole had been dug by Russian prisoners, as a crude open latrine. The opportunity to walk or for some, to stumble about, was just what the doctor ordered. Our sick and wounded had to be helped and they seemed to be improved by the temporary relief.

After dusk, our trucks were coupled to another engine and we again suffered the constant buffeting and clashing, this time for about six hours. By daylight we had reached the city of Leipzig.

Those who had gulped their food down quickly were now very hungry and they cast envious eyes as those of us who had been more prudent as we ate our daily portion.

Again we were allowed out, but for a longer period this time. It was a sunny day and our spirits were raised as a result of this liberty. All day, and all the next night, we waited at Leipzig.

Early on the morning of the 4th September, 1943, our trucks were attached to a lone engine and after crossing a wide river, we arrived at a siding near a very large barbed-wire compound. We were ordered to climb down from the cattle trucks and were counted by the Luftwaffe feldwebel and again by an unteroffizier in a green Wehrmacht uniform. The Luftwaffe guards left us and as we shuffled towards the barbed wire, I saw the name above large wooden entrance gates - M.Stammlager IVB.

THE POST CARD FROM THE AUTHOR TO HIS MOTHER.

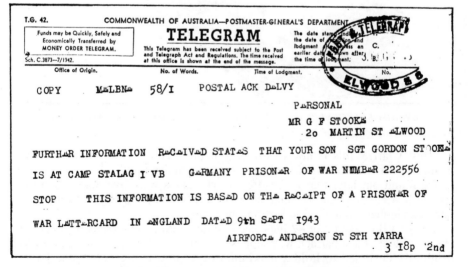

THE OFFICIAL TELEGRAM TO THE AUTHOR'S
MOTHER ADVISING HER THAT HE WAS ALIVE AND A P.O.W.

CHAPTER 9

STAMMLAGER IV B

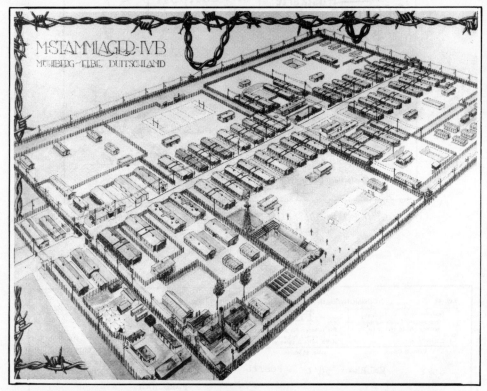

KREIGSGEFANGENERLAGEN M-STAMMLAGER IVB MUHLBURG AM ELBE -
DEUTSCHLAND

"Hey, Clarrie, this is not a Luftwaffe camp." Norm said, alarmed. "The guards are Wehrmacht. We should have gone to a Stalag Luft."

We found out later that Luftwaffe P.O.W. camps were overloaded and the special R.A.F. compound at Stammlager IVB, Muhlburg-am-Elbe, Saxony, was one of a number established in Wehrmacht camps.

Stalag IVB consisted of 42 huts, each divided into two barracks by a central ablution block. Each barrack was supposed to house 180 men, so the camp was originally designed to hold a maximum of 15,000 Kriegsgefangene [war-prisoners]. As well as 'cook houses', there were two hospital huts and a block of 'cooler' cells for misbehavers. At the west entrance were the German army barracks and an ablution block for delousing newcomers. A road ran straight through the centre of the camp from west to east.

Until then Stalag IVB had been occupied by French, Polish and Russian soldiers, along with Serbian and Croatian partisans. Not only were we the first British prisoners brought into the camp but we were the first Air Force captives that these German guards had encountered and were somewhat of a novelty.

After our hungry, sick, tired and filthy band passed through the Wooden Gates of Limbo, we were turned right towards the ablution block. If I had known then what I know now of concentration camps such as Auschwitz, Belsen and Dachau, I would have reeled back in terror on sighting the boiler room and the tall smoking chimney of Stalag IVB's ablution block. Terror would have quickly given way to despair on being ordered to undress and enter the shower room. The only difference between Stalag IVB's ablution block and the abominations at Auschwitz and Belsen were, thankfully, hot water came down from our ceiling nozzles rather than cyanide gas. But at the time, we were not concerned, knowing nothing of Hitler's murderous intent to slaughter and incinerate millions of Jewish people.

After a hot shower our clothes were returned, stinking of carbolic, an unpleasant reminder of Fresnes prison. The smell soon faded or maybe we just became used to it.

Two Russian P.O.W.s were busy preparing a contraption not unlike a sheep shearing machine. With one pedalling and the other shaving, one by one we were relieved of our crowning glory. It fell to the ground severed and unwanted. Even in our unhappy state, the ceremony caused some merriment.

Next we were fingerprinted and photographed, criminal-style, our 'kriegsgefangennummers' hanging around our necks. With documentation

THE MAIN GATE OF M-STAMMLAGER IVB.

THE AUTHOR AFTER BEING ATTENDED
TO BY HIS RUSSIAN BARBER.

RSM J. SMITH, A COSSACK OFFICER
AND W.O. JACK (SNOWSHOES) MEYERS.

complete, we shuffled down the central road to a compound especially prepared for us.

As we passed the barracks fronting the main road, we were shocked and saddened by what we saw. Our state of exhaustion was bad enough but the sight of hundreds of ghostly, pallid faces, many framed in hoods fashioned from blankets and draped in filthy remnants of uniforms, was a wretched and frightening introduction to Stalag IVB. Even in summer, these once proud Russian soldiers wore everything they owned to avoid theft. Heads down in despair, they shuffled about aimlessly when not submitting to the needs of their masters. These poor starving souls were the remains of Russian armies overrun by the German Blitzkriegs of 1940-41. At the gates of Stalingrad, 1,000,000 soldiers were captured. Only 6000 eventually returned to Russia while hunger, brutality, sickness and the cold killed most of them.

Set back from the road in front of our compound was a cookhouse and store. We were marched through barbed wire gates and into the northern barrack of one of four buildings in the enclosure. There was a crude latrine to the right of the entrance door for night use only. Along the left side were 10 sets of 18 bunks - 'lebensraum' for 180 men. Two six foot long wood-fired hotplates, one at either end, were connected by a horizontal brick chimney, its impossible task being to warm the whole area. On the right was a clear 'recreational' space measuring about 10 x 60 feet.

Scrambling for the preferred bunks, Clarrie and I managed to get two top positions, with Norm directly underneath. We filled our palliasses with straw

AN ARTIST'S IMPRESSION OF A STALAG HUT INTERIOR

Prisoners of War will be fired on without warning

(I) IF THEY LEAVE THEIR BARRACKS AFTER LAST POST AND BEFORE REVEILLE.

(II) IF THEY TOUCH OR CROSS THE TRIP-WIRE OR THE FENCE DURING DAYTIME.

THE GERMAN SENTRIES ARE INSTRUCTED TO USE THEIR ARMS IN CASE OF INSUBORDINATION.

THE CAMP COMMANDANT. . . . .

A GRIM REMINDER TO PRISONERS IN THE STALAG

from bales dumped in the compound and were issued with a stiff horsehair blanket, a pannikin and a spoon. So it was, that the crew of D-Donald, in one kriegsgefangenlager or another, began their subsistence as guests of Nazi Germany.

Our day commenced with reveille at 0600 hours in summer, 0700 hours in winter, "Raus, raus, schnell, schnell," yelled the guards, stomping through the barracks, merrily hitting the bed ends with their batons. The smart ones among us were already up in anticipation and on the way out to attend the morning parade. Others dragged themselves out of their bunks with their horsehair blankets over their heads in pious fashion. This was to provide protection from the cold and an attempt to shut out the unacceptability of the situation in which they found themselves.

Forming us up in fives, the Feldwebel marched quickly along our columns and with wagging finger, counted loudly, "funf, zehn, funfzehn, zwanzig, funfundzwanzig," and so on. After consultation with the recently elected British barrack leader, he dismissed us. Many went back to bed. One poor fellow stayed in his bunk for almost two years, shutting himself off from the cruel world that had engulfed him. From time to time, he was dragged out and forceably washed.

Soon after the morning count, buckets of acorn coffee arrived. Breakfast! After a while, this vile-tasting liquid actually began to be in demand.

The rest of the mornings dragged by with cautious walks around our small compound or attending to the call of nature, some often and desperately, in the solid brick latrine in the centre of the compound. Inside, two rows of six round, open holes permitted unrestricted conversation if you felt like a friendly chat but it was hell for those who valued their privacy on such occasions. The smell of lime and human contributions coming up through the holes was overwhelming, but lessened when you sat down.

When full, the sewage from our compound and all latrines in Stalag IVB, was pumped out into special latrine carts by the unfortunate 'Russkis'. It was then disposed of in the surrounding fields, from which came our potatoes. The carts' pungent fumes were to be avoided as they and the Russkis, passed through the camp.

Around midday, potatoes and soup arrived. The potatoes were dirty and the soup was only one or two thicknesses above water. When there was a shortage of 'kartoffel' [potatoes], the few available were thrown in and were found bobbing around in the soup.

Later in the day, sour bread and on rare occasions, 'luxuries' like cheese, sugar and jam [all ersatz] were issued. At no time did the Germans provide the quantity of food agreed to with the Red Cross. For example, we were supposed to get 334 grams of bread per day but I do not believe we ever received even half the agreed ration.

"Lights out" was 2000 hours and so, fully dressed and covered by my crude horsehair blanket, I slept fitfully. I shivered with cold even though it was summer and dreaded the coming winter. I was frequently awakened by my 140-odd fellow 'kriegies' as they collectively snorted, snored, groaned, yelled, moaned and screamed the whole night through. A week later a second group of airmen from Dulag Luft arrived, filling our barrack and overflowing into the southern half of the building.

A week later there was talk of a third batch and sure enough, at about 1400 hours, we watched them march hairless, into the R.A.F. compound. Suddenly, amazed, I recognised a familiar face.

"Stoby, you old bastard," I yelled excitedly.

He grinned back at me from under his Russki haircut. "Stooke, what are you doing here?" he called in recognition, "I thought you were dead."

I had known Bert Stobart at school and he lived in Brighton, Victoria, close to my home. We were both on 19 Course at the R.A.A.F. Initial Training School, Victor Harbour, South Australia. He hardly had time to find himself a bunk before I closed in.

"Any news of home? What squadron were you on? When did you cop it? What happened? Were you wounded?" Questions came faster than Bert could answer.

"Cripes, hang on until I sit down will you?" Bert pleaded.

He had been posted to 460 Squadron just after I was shot down as Rear-Gunner to Flight Sergeant R. B. McPhan. On the 3rd of September, they were detailed to attack Berlin but were intercepted by a fighter over Holland. Bert said the attack seemed to come from the front of the aircraft but later, on reflection, he admitted it could have come from below. Although Bert's Lancaster was severely damaged, he and his Mid Upper-Gunner, Jock Hilton, escaped through the rear door. Sadly all five of his crew mates in the front of the aircraft, were killed.

I have often wondered if Bert's attacker could have been Major Heinz-Wolfgang Schnaufer, 'The Night Ghost of St.Trond', who I described earlier and who was reputed to have shot down over 100 British heavy bombers.

On the 22nd September, 1943 we received from America our first Red Cross Parcel. It contained 12 ounces Meat Roll, 12 ounces Bully Beef, Salmon, Sardines plus biscuits, margarine, powdered milk, sugar, raisins, cheese-spread, concentrated orange, chocolate, coffee and 60 cigarettes. Morale immediately rose sky-high. It was the first good food that Clarrie, Norm and I had eaten for over two months. That night there was almost a party atmosphere in the barracks.

It was amazing how a few days of good food cured even the worst cases of dysentery. The more sensible prisoners, portioned out their food on a day by day basis, while a few woofed the lot and vomited, wastefully. Those best off were the non-smokers because they could buy extra food with their cigarettes. Many German guards could be bribed to bring loaves of bread from Muhlburg-am-Elbe for a few cigarettes. Anything and everything was exchanged by the Germans for blocks of chocolate.

Wonder upon wonders, three days later on the 25th September, 1943, a second American parcel arrived and this time it included 100 cigarettes. During the next two months, issues of food parcels and cigarettes became irregular, resulting in either a famine or a feast. Nevertheless we averaged one parcel per week so were not too badly off.

RUSSIAN PRISONERS HUNTING FOR FOOD
IN DISCARDED FOOD PARCEL TINS - 1945.

In late September, we were joined by a dozen Australian airmen who had been prisoners of the Italians. They described how, when Italy capitulated in September 1943, their Prisoner of War camp, PG 57 at Udine in northern Italy, was surrounded by German troops. Both the Italian guards and the Prigionieri di Guerra were transported to Germany, thence to Stalag IVB, to become Kriegsgefangeners.

One of the newcomers was W/O. G. J. (Gus) Officer. In 1942 Gus was flying his Kittyhawk out of Amiriya, Egypt and on the 3rd of November, he successfully escorted a squadron of British and American medium bombers to their target. On the way back, he was jumped by a flight of Luftwaffe Me109s [beware of the Hun in the sun]. In the dog fight that followed, he was hit by cannon fire, wounded and only just escaped from his crippled Kittyhawk by parachute. Captured by the Germans, Gus was handed over to the Italians and taken to Italy. Persistent pain from his wounds was aggravated by being moved around various camps in southern and northern Italy.

Accompanying Gus to our camp, were personalities such as Jock Watson, Sandy Jones, Alex Richardson, Frank Beste, Jim Churchill, Keith Dodd and Jack Bell, all R.A.A.F. men.

We had elected W/O Jack (Snowshoes) Meyers, R.C.A.F., a Canadian, as our

'Man of Confidence', an onerous job as he was our only contact with the German Kommandant. Snowshoes also represented the British prisoners whenever people from the International Red Cross visited the Stalag.

Before the arrival of the British, the Germans had demanded complete submission within the Stalag. The unfortunate Russians they dominated had long ago, been downtrodden to the point of losing their will to resist. Hunger, sickness and then death seemed their bleak future. They were easy to bring to heel.

Then the Germans were confronted with a compound full of comparatively healthy, well-organised British airmen. Through Snowshoes Myers, they applied to have one of the barracks put aside as a theatre, they wanted huts to conduct educational lectures and they needed space for soccer and cricket pitches. Not only that, they had the affrontery to dig escape tunnels.

The escape committee's first tunnel was discovered when the latrine cart, heavily laden, ran over it and caused a cave in. The Jerries dealt with its discovery very effectively, filling the tunnel with the contents of the cart.

Out of the blue, for several weeks, food parcels were opened and the contents of cans emptied into our pannikins. Whether the German Kommandant was fearful that we might hoard tins of food as escape supplies or whether it was just out of pure spite, we never found out. Whatever the reason, it can be imagined what an unpalatable mix beef stew and jam, covered with powdered milk, made. Later the order was rescinded and the cans were just punctured. Eventually the whole thing was forgotten and we went back to receiving unopened parcels.

I can still see a certain Feldwebel, pickaxe in hand, searching the barracks for unpunctured cans. Whenever he found one he gleefully yelled "Ho! Ho!" as his pickaxe went to work. Everybody in the barrack echoed, in chorus, "Ho! Ho!".

He was, naturally, nicknamed "Pickaxe Pete".

British and American Prisoners of War in Germany were beholden to the International Red Cross for the protection of health and dignity. Without the I.R.C., we would not have survived on German rations alone. Prisoners from countries who had not been signatories at the Geneva Convention of 1864, received no aid from that organisation. Contrary to the Convention, the food rations supplied by the Germans, were never sufficient to sustain life. If they had not been supplemented by the Red Cross, we would have fared no better than the starving Russkis.

The International Red Cross not only supplied us with extra food and clothing but also put us in a position to bribe the German guards. Without doubt, we all owed our lives to the International Red Cross.

Gus Officer and his companions were not the only P.O.W.s to join us from Italy. British army N.C.Os. captured in Egypt and South African troops taken in Tobruk filled a nearby compound. Ironically, thousands of Hitler's former allies, the gallant soldiers of Italy, poured into Stalag IVB to become the most subjugated captives of all.

In the meantime another group of aircrew arrived from Dulag Luft. I moved amongst them, keen to meet Australians, especially if they were from 460 Squadron or Melbourne. I sighted the dark blue uniform of an Australian pilot, who introduced himself as Geoff Taylor of 207 Squadron. Although I had never met Geoff, I did know of him and his family and like Stoby, he lived in Brighton, not far from my home. He told me that, after attacking Hanover on the 18th October, 1943, his Lancaster was fired on by a Luftwaffe Fw 190. The German pilot did his job much too well and soon Z-Zebra was plummeting, out of control, towards the ground. Geoff gamely made sure that all his crew had bailed out safely before he left the now-useless controls to follow them. Before the war, he had been a journalist, so it was not surprising when, shortly after his return home, he wrote "A Piece of Cake" describing his experiences. It makes compelling reading.

By November it was getting very cold and December brought the first of the winter snows. Day time was only just bearable as we crowded around a stove always short of fuel or trudged around and around the compound in an attempt to coax a little warmth back into chilly bones. If the days were cold, then the nights were frigid in the extreme. We huddled under our useless horsehair blankets, fully dressed in every article of clothing we possessed and shivered the night away. But some were worse off. Imagine the intolerable distress in the Russian compound, with no wood for fires and little food or clothing for emaciated bodies.

The British Man of Confidence, Snowshoes Meyers, had already sent an urgent signal to the I.R.C., Switzerland, for clothing and it was his assurance of delivery, plus the issue of an English Christmas parcel, that made the cold more bearable over the 'festive' season.

Each month, the Germans issued us with two postcards and one letter form, with most used to write home but I did send a card to friends in England. It took over six months for replies to come back from Australia [first reply, end of March, 1944] and four months back from England [mid February, 1944].

Letters were not the only way we received news from outside the wire. The two Berlin daily newspapers, the 'Volkischer Beobachter' and the 'Deutsche Allgemeine Zeitung' presented a distorted picture when reporting on the progress of the war. The English language, German-produced newspaper 'The Camp', represented a biased viewpoint of P.O.W. life.

Completely authentic, though, was the wall newspaper, 'News Flash'. This amazing example of P.O.W. ingenuity and artistry was written by journalists such as Geoff Taylor. Multiple copies were meticulously hand-written, by scribes, one copy for each barrack. Even more extraordinary was the source of the news read out by Taffy Harris each night between 2000 and 2100 hours. The cry of "B.B.C. news up" demanded immediate silence, as Taffy read from his notes. The genius shown by Sgt. E. R. Gargini to hand-build a radio receiver, hide it in a gramophone case and each day listen to the B.B.C., London, news broadcast, was amazing. He bribed guards for some parts and wound R.F. and A.F. coils and transformers by hand. He put these crude bits and pieces together in secret to construct an efficient radio. Much was owed to the skills and patience of men such as he.

Eventually the camp Kommmandant gave approval for us to convert one of the barracks into a theatre. So in January, 1944, after much hard work, the

AN ARTIST'S IMPRESSION OF THE
CAMP MAIN STREET IN WINTER

"Empire Theatre" was opened with the presentation of "The Muhlburg Melody of 1944". This musical was judged by those who know, to be of world class. Musical instruments were supplied by the Red Cross and clothing, props., etc., made in the camp. It ran for over a week and was seen by all British Kriegies and German officers.

During November, December and January, cold continued to be enemy number one. Even enjoyment of our new theatre was put to the test by the cold as it permeated everything. So when it was announced that a clothing issue was imminent, spirits soared.

Each man received a British army greatcoat, a pullover and a pair of strong leather boots, again all thanks to the Red Cross.

Shortly after this I received a personal parcel sent from England by Mr. Jack

Hewitt, my father's friend. Inside was a woollen balaclava, a pair of woollen gloves, socks and long-johns. Now, I was certainly well set up for next winter - if we were still here! Jack Hewitt also arranged for cigarettes to be sent to me fortnightly. This was the same as sending cash, as mentioned earlier, cigarettes were the currency of the camp. The trouble was I smoked, so all day long I was literally setting 'legal' tender on fire.

On the 9th March, 1944 I 'celebrated' my majority. From this day on I would be a man amongst men, a person of note. The day before, was I not a no-account, frivolous youth, harebrained, irresponsible? Not true!! My youth had been lost long ago.

Also in March an outbreak of typhus and diphtheria made quarantining necessary so inter-barrack visiting was restricted - bringing activities to a standstill. The quarantine lasted five weeks, so each barrack had to find its own entertainment. One night, I contributed with an exhibition boxing match with Brummy, a hard-boiled lad from Birmingham. We arranged beforehand to take it easy but it seemed that Brummy did not get the message. He clobbered me twice with hard, swinging rights to the head and I was hard-put to keep him at bay, even with my practised hard straight lefts. I vowed never to give 'exhibition' bouts from then on. The funny thing about boxing is that generally you become good pals with your opponent as I did with Brummy - something to do with mutual respect.

Probably the most popular game played in the camp was contract bridge and my constant partner was John [Doc] Haines, an Australian from Gosford, N.S.W. We played in-barrack, inter-barrack, inter-services and later, international bridge against French, Danish and Dutch prisoners. We used the Blackwood Convention and although we never won a top competition, we became pretty good and claimed our share of the stakes [cigarettes].

Once, when collecting a cigarette parcel at the camp post office, I noticed that the German postal officer had, for security reasons, unwrapped a parcel sent to a British soldier. It was a child's 'Bobs' set complete with wooden cue, wooden ball and a wooden set of ten openings to aim at. It seemed a silly toy to send an adult. Even worse, over each door was a photograph of Hitler, Goebbels, Goering, Mussolini, etc. How stupid to send such a thing to Germany. If the postal official had been a hard-line Nazi, there could well have been trouble. What an insult, aiming balls at 'der Fuhrer'. But it seems he was not a hard-liner and merely said, "Wo es Churchill und Roosevelt?" and with a smile handed over the ridiculous gift.

Red Cross parcels were adequate during Spring, 1944 and they prompted the would-be epicureans in our midst to dream up some amazing concoctions. For example, directly they opened their food parcels, some indulgent Kriegies would have a 'Klim-Bash' [Klim - powdered milk - milk spelt backwards.]
KLIM-BASH. Method:- Add water to Klim, mix to a paste and then devour.
ANGELS' FOOD. Method:- As for Klim-Bash, except add packet of raisins and, maybe, grated chocolate. Devour the lot.
BURGOO. Method:- Grate Canadian biscuits into a powder and add a heaped spoonful of Klim and sugar. Boil a pint of water, add the dry mixture and allow

A GERMAN JU88 "BUZZING" THE P.O.W. CAMP.

to simmer for two minutes. Add half a spoonful of butter and allow to cool. It was supposed to turn out like blanc-mange. These were just a few of the concoctions.

Amongst us were quite a few professional master chefs probably army cooks. An organised display of their culinary skills showed an impressive adaptability. Considering the ingredients came from Red Cross food parcels and were prepared in a P.O.W camp, their array of decorated cakes and other delights was fascinating. Their handy work was a mouth-watering, sight for sore eyes.

On April 30th, 1944 we witnessed the tragic, accidental death of Sgt. Herbert Mallory, R.C.A.F, a Lancaster pilot who had earlier been shot down on a raid on Nuremberg on 27th August, 1943. He came from New Brunswick, Canada. For some time, trainee Luftwaffe pilots from Lonnewitz airfield, just north of Stalag IVB, had been buzzing our camp. It is likely they knew that there were R.A.F aircrew prisoners inside and like young trainees everywhere, they welcomed the opportunity to show off their skills, especially to enemy counterparts. As their Ju 88s came over the camp at tree-top level, our signals enticed them to fly lower and lower. We hoped that, with a bit of luck, one of them might have pranged. The show was enjoyed by both the Deutscher Luftwaffe and the Royal Air Force.

Herb was walking around the south compound with his buddy, Wally Massey, a fellow 'Canuck'. One of the Ju 88s came in so low that a propeller hit Herb on the head as it flashed by at 250 kilometres per hour, killing him instantly.

This was disgraceful airmanship on the part of the young Luftwaffe pilot, as his propeller tips must have been only five feet above the ground. Even the most inexperienced pilot would not risk his life by flying so low.

I can still see that Ju 88, climbing away, with barbed wire from the eastern fence, caught in its tail wheel. We heard later, that the pilot was court-martialled, reduced to the ranks and sent to the Russian front. The Charge - 'Endangering property of the Reich.'

Rumours were around that something big was about to happen. The B.B.C. had been uncharacteristically quiet, then on June 7th, 1944, we read the headlines in the Deutsche Allgemeine Zeitung, the whole camp was agog. "Die Invasion hat begonnen," [the invasion has begun] the Berlin newspaper announced promptly. This landing, the Italian front and the Russian offensive in the East, meant that the Nazis were fighting for survival on three fronts. We would be home for Christmas, for sure. I celebrated by attending a splendid presentation of 'The Man Who Came to Dinner' at the Empire Theatre.

Then we heard of the attempt on Hitler's life at his Wolfslair in Rastenberg. First reports were that he had been killed but we later learnt that the attempt by Claus von Stauffenberg had only wounded him. It would not have been surprising if the plotters had met their end in front of a firing squad. However, der Fuhrer planned a grislier end and these very senior officers were garrotted with piano wire. The maniac had his revenge.

When Paris fell to the Allies on the 24th August, we were convinced that the war would soon be over. How wrong we were.

A few British, American and Canadian troops, captured during the invasion, begin to trickle in. They were in very bad condition, some having taken over a month to get here. Soon the trickle became a steady stream, putting a strain on our dwindling stocks of food parcels. It looked as though we would soon have to rely on German rations again.

During September and October we had a dearth of Red Cross parcels and distribution dropped to half a parcel, per man, per week - most worrying considering the onset of winter. The shortage was brought about primarily by the constant Allied bombing of the German railway system.

In early October the remnants of operation 'Market Garden' arrived at Stalag IVB. This operation was quoted as being the most spectacular, yet tragic, episode of the allied advance towards Germany. The British paratroopers' attack on Arnhem in Northern Holland was an utter disaster. Field-Marshal Montgomery had submitted a plan to seize Arnhem, in northern Holland, using paratroopers and glider commandos. After reinforcement, they were supposed to strike towards the Zuider Zee, so encircling 400,000 German troops in the Low Countries - a brilliant plan to speed the end of the war. The U.S. 82 and 101st Airborne Divisions and the British 1st Airborne Division were to be used. With absolute control of the air, the operation commenced on September 17th. Vital bridges at Arnhem were overrun by the British and these they held awaiting the arrival of the 2nd Army, still 60 miles to the south. They repulsed constant counter-attacks by German Storm Troopers and Panzer squadrons. Unfortunately the strength of the Germans in the area had been under-estimated and it also began to rain, pouring for four days. The 2nd army was bogged down and could not advance as planned and the paratroopers at Arnhem lost their air cover because of the overcast. Of the 10,000 men who landed at Arnhem, only

2400 made it back to Allied lines.

A tribute came from a most unexpected source when Berlin radio reluctantly reported that the British 'fought tenaciously'. Indeed they did, those courageous men of Arnhem. If the wretched condition of the paratroopers, 'lucky' enough to be captured, was indicative of the gallantry of their resistance for ten days and nights, then 'spectacular' and 'tragic' are understatements. Muddy, wet, exhausted and hungry, supporting their walking wounded, they stumbled through the main gates of the Stalag.

Towards the end of November, 1944, winter nights and the pangs of hunger returned. These conditions were not good for the old inhabitants of Stalag IVB but so much worse for the newer inmates, as yet unaccustomed to the rigours of P.O.W. life.

We awoke one morning to find the compound next to ours occupied by 1000 Polish women. Captured in Warsaw when Poland's courageous 'Operation Storm' finally came to its bitter end on October 21st, their arrival certainly caused a buzz of excitement throughout the camp.

As the Russian army approached Warsaw, the 40,000 strong Polish Home Army and civilians rose up and for 63 bloody days, opposed the might of the German Wehrmacht. 15,000 Poles died along with 10,000 Germans. The Polish Lt-General Tadeusz Komorowski was finally forced to surrender because the Russians, although close at hand, refused to help. They were still smarting over a previous disagreement with the exiled Polish Government, a petty argument that cost thousands of brave Poles their lives.

After a couple of days, the Polish women left our camp to die in concentration camps or to otherwise perform whatever degenerate tasks their Nazi masters required of them.

Christmas 1944 led to a depressed January, 1945. Food parcels had run out and Allied armies on both the eastern and western fronts had come to a stop. Not only that, rumours of a German offensive in the west were confirmed with the arrival of captured American soldiers from the 'Battle of the Bulge'. On December 15th, a desperate Hitler had played his last card with his plan to drive a wedge between the Allied forces and recapture Antwerp. Secretly he had reinforced his armies in the Ardennes and on December 16th, under the command of Field-Marshal Walther Model, an attack was launched. Under cover of thick fog and snow, 26 German divisions overwhelmed 6 unsuspecting divisions of the U.S. 1st Army. The size of the attack rivalled the Allied invasion of France on 6th June. The Germans drove a 25 mile wide wedge into Belgium and by December 21st had almost reached Liege. On December 26th the skies cleared, allowing the R.A.F and the U.S.A.A.F to attack the German divisions. General Patton's Third Army advanced to relieve the heroic American Airborne Division besieged in Bastogne. By January all lost ground had been recovered and the 'Battle of the Bulge' was over. In the meantime 20,000 American troops had been taken prisoner. Those who were herded into Stalag IVB were in a condition as bad as the men from Arnhem.

Expecting the new Americans to have tales to tell, I hot footed it down to their barracks. It was not a pretty sight as the barrack had already been full of

British soldiers when 100s of Americans were crammed in on top of them. The Yanks were lying on the floor between the bunks and filling the 'recreational' area. Many were wounded and being attended to by their buddies. They had not been fed for a week or so and we had little or nothing to give them. One was Lou Phelper from Cleveland, Ohio and I spent time chatting with him and another G.I. I got along well with both of them, particularly Lou. I told them of my experiences over the last year or so and they told me what happened in the Ardennes. They confirmed that the Americans were few and raw whilst the Germans were many and seasoned. They told me that English speaking Germans, dressed in Yank uniforms, infiltrated their lines. Intriguing!

On February 13/14th the unscathed ancient city of Dresden was targeted once by the R.A.F. and five times by the U.S.A.A.F. This devastating attack had political ramifications that I do not intend to comment on. The raid affected Stalag IVB and other R.A.F./U.S.A.A.F. camps because of a rumour that an enraged Hitler was seeking his revenge on all airmen P.O.W.s. We were to be stood in front of a firing squad and shot in retaliation. True or not, frightening reports of this kind naturally resulted in a wave of anxiety running through the camp. Later, it was reported that the Fuhrer's generals suppressed the order.

During February even the inadequate German rations were cut. I felt hungrier than in Fresnes and one-eighth of a Red Cross parcel per week was of little help. I did get a cigarette parcel from England, sent six months previously by George Apperley [father of Joy Apperley, who was to become my wife]. I traded some for bread and smoked the rest.

One afternoon, as I talked to Geoff Taylor, he surprised me by saying that he had been out of the camp. His story was well-nigh unbelievable and if it had not him telling it, I would have thought my leg was being pulled. He planned had been to seize an aircraft from Lonewitz airfield and fly to Sweden. Bribery could get you anywhere in war-time Germany and complete details of the Ju 88's cockpit layout cost Geoff a carton of cigarettes and three blocks of chocolate.

One day in February, 1945, he and Smithy, his Canadian bomb-aimer, left the camp dressed as French workers, carrying forged copies of all the necessary paperwork. So that they would look like genuine busy workers, they picked up a length of timber and carried it on their shoulders. On reaching Lonewitz, they waited for the right moment and then walked onto the aerodrome, lying low near where aircraft were dispersed.

At about 1900 hours, a Ju 88 landed and pulled up near them. The crew got out, and were driven away while the aircraft was refuelled.

"Perfect. Hot engines and full of petrol," Geoff told Smithy.

Just after dark, they crept over to the aircraft, opened the hatch and climbed in. Seated in the cockpit, Geoff took only a moment to look over the controls. His finger was on the starter button when somebody yelled, in German. "Was machst du da drien?" [What are you doing in there?] Luckily Smithy was bi-lingual as his parents were Canadian/German. Understanding, he replied in German. "We're cold, we were going to sleep in here."

"Komme mal daraus," roared the voice, "schnell, schnell." [Come out, quickly, quickly.]

Scrambling out they saw that the voice belonged to a Luftwaffe guard. As amazing as it seems, the guard believed them and did nothing more than send them on their way. So they picked up their length of timber and walked off Lonewitz aerodrome. They then waited until the morning before footing it back to Stalag IVB like two stop-outs returning home after a night out on the town.

I still wonder how many airmen attempted to commandeer an enemy aircraft during wartime, as Geoff and Smithy tried to do. I believe they elected themselves to a very exclusive club which included Douglas Bader as a member.

I wonder too, how many acts of pure courage by P.O.W.s, such as Geoff's and Smithy's, went unrewarded. Unhappily too many!! In 'A Piece of Cake', Geoff Taylor gives a detailed account of this courageous attempt.

During all of March 1945 we received only half a food parcel per man. The German ration was now down to a quarter of that prescribed by the Geneva Convention. The Russian army was very close and this was surely the beginning of the end for Germany. Even the guards admitted it.

"Deutschland kaput," [Germany finished,] they whimpered, red eyed.

One morning as I was walking to the latrine, I half-heard, half-felt the 'splat-splat-splat' of bullets landing all around me. Then, almost at the same time , I heard the 'rat-tat-tat' of machine gun fire as an American low flying P51 Mustang roared over. Too late to reach cover, I hit the dirt and when I opened my eyes, I saw a 0.5 bullet clip a foot from my head. I reached out and picked it up and still have it.

This attack on what they thought was a German military target, cost the lives of one Englishman, two Dutchmen and three Russians - all Kriegys, with one German guard wounded. We cursed the bungling U.S.A.A.F. intelligence officer who failed to brief his pilots properly. This was not the only strafing attack by 'friendly' aircraft. The camp slowly filled up with forced labour workers from surrounding farms while others had been force-marched from camps to the east. By the end of March there were 50,000 prisoners, representing dozens of nationalities, in Stalag IVB.

During the night of the 21st/22nd April we heard the chatter of machine-gun fire. Then the boom, boom of heavier guns in the distance. Sleep was impossible. Something was about to happen.

Next morning the German guards were gone, the machine gun towers empty and a murmur that grew into a roar, spread through the camp. Some scenes I will remember forever. Russian prisoners, who yesterday had been dragging one foot after the other, took the wire in their stride and in their thousands, headed east at a gallop as if Moscow was just over the next hill.

We expected to see the Russian army, automatic weapons at the ready, supported by dozens of tanks and armoured cars, hurrying from the east to free us. Instead, at 1000 hours, across the fields came three lonely Cossacks, on horseback. What an anti-climax.

Stammlager IVB, Muhlburg-am-Elbe, Saxony had been liberated.

CHAPTER 10

THE RUSSIANS AND THE AMERICANS

RSM J. SMITH, A COSSACK OFFICER AND WO JACK (SNOWSHOES) MEYERS AFTER THE LIBERATION OF STALAG IVB - 1945.

The three Cossacks trotted down the main road of the camp and back again, showed little interest and went on their way. For the rest of the day the British and American ex-'Kriegys' waited, expecting help and direction from our Russian deliverers.

Late that afternoon, two Russian officers arrived in a Jeep but after a short conference with Snowshoes Meyers, they also left. We knew then that we could not expect any help from the Russian army. They had nothing to give as they were used to living off the land as they advanced, and it seemed they expected us to do the same.

It was best not to think of the dreadful fate of the local German farmers, with 50,000 vindictive, starving P.O.W.'s and the Russian army, both ravaging the countryside - and other Germans, for that matter.

Lou Phelper, the survivor from the Battle of the Bulge and I, planned to walk to the local villages of Burxdorf and Saxdorf to look for food. We started out early the next day, heading first for Burxdorf. As Lou and I approached the nearby railway line, we saw a group of Russian soldiers amusing themselves taking pot-shots with their rifles, at the overhead porcelain telephone insulators.

"Amerikaner, Englander," we quickly told them before they took pot shots at us.

More pot shots were fired at the insulators before a Russian officer arrived on a motor cycle. After much unintelligible screaming and yelling, he closed the shooting gallery and I could only guess at what he said. I was sure he pointed out that the telephone line was no longer German but Russian, and was even now transmitting vital military information.

The officer went off, happy in the knowledge that he had prevented a breakdown in communications. As soon as he was out of earshot, bang went the rifles again and splat went the insulators, much to the amusement of the marksmen. So much for the discipline, or more to the point, the intellect of the peasant Russian soldier in those days.

We came to the edge of Burxdorf village and after helping another Russian officer to start a motor-cycle he had just found, we invaded a two-storey house nearby. The house was empty and had been looted many times before but I souvenired a German army officer's cap, belts, knives and medals from a bedroom upstairs.

After unsuccessfully searching for food in other abandoned houses in the area, we made our way back to Stalag IVB. We had a sleepless night and again suffered the ever-mounting pain of acute hunger.

The following morning, Lou and I were off to search for food again, but thousands of other hungry British, American, French, Dutch, Serbs and Italians crowded the surrounding countryside, all with the same thing in mind. Nobody expected to find much, as the Russian army had been there before us.

We had walked south for about a mile or so, on a road parallel to the railway, when, menacingly, around a corner came a party of about ten German soldiers. We were about to duck for cover when we saw that two Russians, armed with machine guns, had the Jerries in charge. This was of little comfort to us as we were not too sure of our Russki allies. There was nothing to do but to brazen it out.

"Amerikaner, Englander," Lou called out. I noticed a nervous quiver in his voice.

One of the Russians smiled and indicated that we should join the Germans. Praying that his smile meant he was joking, we cheekily motioned that we had no intention of doing as he suggested. Much to our relief, this was accepted. Wasting no time and fearing that he may change his mind, we went on our way - hurrying slowly! The Russians and their German prisoners, were soon out of sight but not out of earshot. I often reflect on the machine-gun fire I heard and the fate of those German soldiers. Maybe the Russkis were shooting at insulators again!

To our left and about a hundred yards in from the road, we saw a farmhouse and barn, half hidden by trees.

"That looks a likely place," I said, "let's try our luck there."

Lou went to the barn while I tried the house. Before I could even start searching, an excited yell sent me scurrying over to the barn.

"Look what I've found," Lou said triumphantly. He was standing by a sty, ogling a large, fat and juicy pig.

"We can't get that back to camp," I said, "it's too big. It'll get away before we're half way there."

"We'll have to butcher it here," Lou said.

Neither of us had ever killed an animal in our lives. We were both city-born and bred, he in Cleveland, I in Melbourne and normally we might have found it difficult to set a mouse trap. But times were not normal, so we found a large knife in the farmhouse and it was Lou who had the courage to put the beast down. Then, just as we had taken one of the hind quarters, two Frenchmen arrived so we left the rest of the carcass in their care.

Arriving back in camp, we found that Clarrie, Norm and a few others had a fire going and a large boiler was bubbling away. Potatoes found in nearby fields had been added to vegetables taken from surrounding farms. Our contribution of the hind-quarter of a pig was indeed gratefully accepted and ceremonially added to the cauldron. It took much patience and strength of character to wait the four hours it took to cook the pork but the resultant soup was, to starving Kriegys, pure lip-smacking bliss.

Following this sumptuous repast, I slept well, except for attacks of indigestion, nausea, retching, stomach ache and flatulence, not to mention generally feeling just a little off colour.

The number of Kriegies left in Stalag IVB halved during the next few days. After the first day's exodus of the Russkis and the Yugoslavian partisans, along with most of the French and other West Europeans, only the British and the Americans were left. Further scavenging and scrounging was a waste of time as there could have been little left in Saxony, and a very small issue of bread, organised through the Russians, helped somewhat.

Other than food, what concerned us most were the rumours buzzing about; war between America and Russia was imminent; the Russkis intended to take us to Moscow for indoctrination or we were to be taken to Odessa for shipment to England. False though they were, reports of this kind were frightening, especially to those who had been prisoners since the evacuation of Dunkirk, five years before.

We heard that the Russian and American armies had met at Torgau on the Elbe river, about 15 miles north west of Muhlberg. We had already been 'liberated' for over a week and our dwindling patience and the uncertainty about the future, convinced Lou Phelper and me to head for Torgau. I was concerned at leaving Clarrie and Norm but I knew they would understand. And so it was that, early on the 30th April, 1945, Lou and I left Stammlager IVB, Muhlberg am Elbe on foot, heading for Torgau.

On the way we passed many Russian soldiers who were armed to the teeth but they took little notice, and seemed happy to accept us. They must have been told there would be many ex-prisoners about. This was a relief, because our greatest concern, was what their attitude would be towards two foreigners wandering around on ground recently won with the blood of their comrades.

The city of Torgau was on the west side of the river Elbe and we arrived on the east side at about three o'clock in the afternoon. The Torgau bridge had been destroyed but a temporary pontoon bridge was under construction. We were told it would be finished within a day or so, so we made ourselves comfortable in a nearby deserted farmhouse.

There were still a few chickens running around the farmyard with 'eat me' written all over them. The trouble was they would not stay still long enough to be caught. After about five minutes trying to grab one by its tail, we gave up. Then we noticed two Russian soldiers watching our performance, both grinning like Cheshire cats. One of them picked up a stick and as a luckless chicken ran by, he struck its legs. When it stopped rolling, he picked it up, wrung its neck and handed it to me. The look on his face clearly said, "where have you been all your life, you imperialistic bird-brain?" Using much sign-language, a little German and even less Russian and English, we made arrangements for the two soldiers to be back at seven o'clock. By then the bird would be cooked and ready to eat, along with some potatoes we had found. There was much more to preparing the chicken than we thought. Our plucking left many feathers behind and cleaning it ended up as a not-too-successful surgical operation.

We found a boiler, fired the stove and after an hour's cooking, chicken and potatoes were ready for our visitors. They arrived on time and with much merriment the meal was consumed.

"Zigarette?" I asked when we had finished.

One reached into his greatcoat pocket and proudly produced a handful of powdery, loose tobacco.

"Papier?" I inquired. His hand went back into his pocket.

"Newspaper!" I turned to Lou in disbelief. "They use newspaper to roll cigarettes."

Not wanting to hurt their feelings, I tried one. The tobacco was bad enough, but add newspaper and one puff was more than an imperialistic bird-brain could stand. I coughed and spluttered violently much to the amusement of the Russkis. Our new friends left at about 9 o'clock and Lou and I settled down for the night.

The following morning, we went to the river to see if the pontoon bridge had been finished. American engineers were still working but it looked as though it would not be ready for a day or so yet. People of all nationalities were trying to get to the American sector across the Elbe river, including German refugees, hoping that the GIs would treat them more kindly than the Russians.

Back at our farmhouse, forever hungry, we searched around and found a few bits of potatoes and turnips in the barn. They were mostly rotten but we were able to sort out and cook a scrappy meal. Many times during that day we had to protect our farmhouse from intruders.

To our surprise and delight, the bridge was finished when we went down to the river next morning, so we crossed the Elbe and entered the city of Torgau.

American soldiers were everywhere and our sense of relief was overwhelming. Until we crossed the Elbe, we had felt restricted and still confined, as liberation by the Russians had been overshadowed by uncertainty. Maybe it was just the language barrier that had made us feel insecure.

Occupied by Americans, Torgau was a completely different situation, as we could speak and be understood. We were with our own kind. No longer were we captive and at last, all the shackles had been removed. We felt as though this defeated city and all that was in it, was ours for the taking. And it was certainly true of the D.K.W. car we found on the side of the road as we made our way towards the centre of town. There was no ignition key and we did not know how to start it until a passing Canadian airman fiddled around under the bonnet and it burst into life. Too late if the car had been booby-trapped!

"Let's drive it to France and sell it," suggested businessman Lou, with an American's instinct for making a Buck.

"What a good idea," I agreed.

"I'll drive," our new Canadian companion said, as I got into the passenger seat, Lou sat in the back and we were off.

We found the Torgau to Leipzig autobahn but after going only a few miles, were stopped by an American sentry.

"You can't drive around in that," he told us. "It hasn't got a white star on the door. You're likely to be shot at by our side and there are still some armed Heinies around as well. You'll have to drive to our Command Post, down there." He pointed down a side road. As we were just about out of petrol, we took his advice.

The Captain at the Command Post was not much interested in us but said we could have petrol. We asked him to paint a star on the side door but he refused but happily sent us on our way.

On the autobahn again we were passed by two Chevy staff cars with General's flags flying from their front mudguards.

"Get behind them," Lou said. "We won't be stopped then." He was right. The sentries, seeing the staff cars, came to attention and presented arms, while enlisted man Lou, had a great time saluting in reply as we raced by in convoy. It was not that easy, as the Chevys were too fast for the DKW so we had trouble pacing them.

"We are doing 70 miles per hour," the Canadian said, "she'll blow up in a minute." The DKW's engine was screaming and that rang a bell in my mind.

"Hey! This engine's a two stroke," I exclaimed, "it should have oil mixed with the petrol. You'd better ease up."

Just after we passed at high speed, through the town of Mockrehna, the Chevys left us behind and were soon out of sight. Inevitably we were stopped again by a sentry.

"I know," Lou said before the soldier could open his mouth. "There are Heinie S.S. troops all around us. We haven't got a star painted on our door and we have to go to the Command Post down that road. Right?"

"Wrong, the C.P. is over there." The sentry pointed in the opposite direction. We did not go to the Command Post but skirted around a bit and got back onto the autobahn and drove into what used to be Eilenberge; now a ghost town. Every building in the town was raised to the ground. The few remaining walls were a hideous reminder of what were once someone's homes. Why would such a small, no consequence town like Eilenburg be annihilated in this way? And what of the townsfolk?

We found out that a company of American GI's had confidently entered the town because white flags of surrender were flying from almost every building. Hiding behind the flags were Nazi S.S. troops in ambush with rifles and machine-guns cocked and ready. At the appropriate moment the unscrupulous Nazi S.S. officer ordered his troops to open fire on the G.I.s.

Hundreds of Americans were killed or wounded, before the survivors quickly pulled out of Eilenburg, and then in anger, unmercifully shelled it into ruin. Finally Sherman tanks entered the town to complete the job. This depravity should never have happened, but who was to blame? The corrupt opportunism of the Nazi S.S. officer or the 'over-reaction' of the Americans? Most of the ordinary people of Eilenburg were beyond caring anyway.

As we neared Leipzig, we were once again stopped by a sentry. This time the Command Post was close at hand but the Captain was not so co-operative. Our car was confiscated and we were trucked into Leipzig to a holding area for ex-prisoners of war. So much for the fortune we were going to make, selling our DKW in France. Late that afternoon we were taken to Halle aerodrome and billeted, while awaiting air transport back to Britain.

At long last, we thought, all our problems were over, with the endless resources of the United States Army available to us. Food would be in abundance and cigarettes galore for the asking, with Bing Crosby and Bob Hope concerts and John Wayne and Gary Cooper movies on every night for our entertainment. Unhappily the cushy life was not to be.

The American generals had fought their way as far east as possible before meeting up with the Russians. Consequently, their advance through Germany to Torgau had been so fast that logistics had been left far behind. Food was severely rationed and the American GI's joined us in bemoaning our aching voids.

Next morning Lou and I decided to walk to the town square in Halle, a mile or so away. In a vain hope, we thought the baker was baking or the hotelier hosting and we had cigarettes to trade. Sadly, most food shops were closed and those that were open had long queues forming outside. Food may well have been our first priority but finding a barber shop ready for business. a haircut, shave and shampoo would be a boost to our dented morale.

The German barber could not speak English but indicated that he was happy to accept cigarettes as payment for his services. Lou went first and after a quarter of an hour, got up from the Wizard's chair a new man. Well, from the neck up anyway.

Then it was my turn and I enjoyed the haircut. But when this meek and mild German barber began to strop his cut-throat razor, my imagination ran riot and as if bewitched, his white coat seemed to change into a Nazi S.S. uniform. When the keen edge of his blade caressed my apprehensive throat, I was sure a fanatical leer spread over his face. What the hell was I doing there? This erstwhile enemy may have already identified me as a British 'terrorflieger' and having lost close relatives in a R.A.F. raid, was about to extract a gory revenge.

My senses must have been numbed with imagined fear, because it seemed only a moment, and it was all done and I was responding to a stimulating shampoo. I found that my jugular was still intact, all was well in Halle. Although I had enjoyed the services of 'Figaro Fritz', I was not sorry to pay him his cigarettes and leave.

After two more days of hunger and boredom, we were told that we were leaving by air the next morning. And so it was that on the 7th May, 1945, I said my farewells to Lou Phelper and with other British Air Force ex-P.O.W.s., boarded a U.S.A.A.F. Dakota and departed German soil.

During the flight across Germany, the navigator of the Dakota told us that our destination was Brussels aerodrome, there to be handed over to the R.A.F. for transport to England.

Just before we reached the Belgian border, the pilot circled around what was left of the city of Cologne and its devastation begged description. We could have

THE COLOGNE CATHEDRAL
TOWERING OVER THE RUINED CITY - 1945

easily been convinced that we were looking down on a huge treeless cemetery. Grotesque tombstone-like bits of buildings were standing in rows that used to be streets. In the centre of this destruction, like a massive mausoleum, stood the apparently undamaged Cologne Cathedral. Protected by providence possibly, but more likely its survival was a tribute to its constructors - plus a large slice of pure and simple luck.

Cologne was only one of dozens of German cities razed during W.W.2. Where was the sense of it all? I hoped that generations to come would benefit from the modern cities that would rise from the ashes of the old. There had to be a legacy because these new cities have cost Germany a generation.

From the Brussels aerodrome, we were taken by British army trucks to a transit depot. There were about forty of us and a scruffier lot you would not find in a day's march. A few wore dirt-encrusted remnants of R.A.F. battle-dress but most, including myself, were dressed in an assortment of bedraggled American army and British army uniforms and civilian clothes. We had not washed for weeks, so even our best friends would not want to know us.

Even so, we were led into a mess hall and sat down at long tables draped with laundry-clean white table cloths. In came mess-orderlies, carrying trays laden with fresh white bread, pure butter and real fruit jam. It is hard to describe the pandemonium that followed. Some started to gulp the fresh bread on its own, not even taking time to spread it with butter. Those who included the butter and jam experienced gastronomic ecstasy. Most of us had been living for years on strictly-rationed portions of sour black bread with occasional unsavoury ersatz margarine. The fare in front of us tasted like cake - no - even better than cake. It was a simple meal by most standards but one I will never forget, especially when the mess-orderlies topped it off with cups of real tea, real milk and real sugar. Their inducement to "Git stuck inta it, lud" brought tears to many eyes.

As we took off the next day in an R.A.F. Dakota, I was reminded of that day, almost two years previously, when I left this same city in the custody of the infamous Captain de Zitter.

Shortly afterwards we crossed the Belgian coast near Dunkerque, now well on our way to R.A.F. Station Westcott, Oxfordshire. I recalled that the last time I had crossed the coast of Europe had been that night in June 1943, as Lancaster UV-D took us to our target at Wuppertal.

For the crew of D-Donald, the "Wake of Wuppertal" would be soon stilled as each of us, in our turn, flew over the white cliffs of Dover towards a new life. A life irreparably changed by our service in Bomber Command and our experiences as guests of the Third Reich.

CHAPTER 11

STRIKE AND RETURN
AN EPILOGUE

The crew of D-Donald endured almost two years of captivity and then spent a short time in England recuperating. At the end of 1945, Clarrie and Norm returned to their wives in Australia and Frank, Rowdy and I had our homecomings with our parents. Dennis and Colin had earlier been reunited with their families in England.

I had met Joy Apperley at a dance in 1940, she being fourteen and I seventeen. We were married in 1946 after I returned to Australia from overseas.

We had three children, two girls and a boy who, in turn, presented us with four grandchildren.

For the next thirty years, I was involved with peripheral equipment in the computer industry and in that capacity travelled overseas on a number of occasions.

I was a very keen yachtsman during that time and took executive office at the Royal Brighton Yacht Club in 1959/60.

With Joy, I returned to Europe during August and September, 1990. We visited Alken in northern Belgium where my Lancaster D-Donald had crashed and burned in Alkerstraat, only 600 metres from the centre of town.

At a civic reception given us by Burgemeester Raymond Jeuris and his councillors, we met many local citizens, some of whom remembered that night in 1943 when Alken came so close to disaster. Mijnheer Luc Smolders acted as a most capable charge d'affaires. I received a treasured gift, an exhaust valve and spring salvaged from one of D-Donald's four Rolls Royce Merlin engines by Mijnheer Josef Huygen and presented to me that day. Josef had kept it for nearly fifty years.

Joy and I retraced my 1943 trek through St.Trond, Gembloux, Charleroi and Binche. With Paolo Smeyers and his wife Jeanne, we returned to the farm at the Abbaye de Bonne Esperance. Paolo had already told us of the death of his mother, Madame Alice Smeyers-Jurion. Nevertheless we were warmly welcomed by her sister, Madame Aline Roshez-Jurion and her husband Maurice. We then visited the home of Jacky Smeyers in nearby Vellereille les Brayeux.

In Paolo's car we followed my bicycle journey from Bonne Esperance to the Chateau de Marteau-Longe, Arbre. Sadly, General and Madame Nicod and Guy and Yannick Bruynoghe had passed away but 'little' Marie-Claire Deflandre-Nicod was there to greet us. Later we visited the tent site on the hill and planted a commemorative oak tree. Next we were honoured at a civic reception by the Bourgmestre de Profondeville, Docteur Jean-Marie Evrard. Shortly after we were pleased to meet Yannick's widow, Margo Bruynoghe. A visit to Brussels followed and the spontaneity of our reception and the success of our stay in Belgium was entirely due to the endeavours of Paolo and Jeanne Smeyers, Marie-Claire Deflandre-Nicod and Luc Smolders.

Piloot Stooke viel in 1943 uit de hemel

47 jaar na de crash terug in Alken

ALKEN — Tijdens de Tweede Wereldoorlog zijn er heel wat vliegtuigen neergestort in Alken. Toen de Geschied- en oudheidkundige Kring van het Brouwersdorp op zoek ging naar informatie over één bepaald toestel, bleken er meer Alkenaren te zijn die erover wisten. Die inlichtingen leidden naar de piloot van de Lancaster bommenwerper, die in de nacht van 24 juni 1943 neerstortte in Alken. 47 jaar na datum kwam de Australiër samen met zijn echtgenote op zoek in Limburg, een onderdeel van zijn twee maanden lange reis doorheen Europa op zoek naar zijn eigen verleden. Met de informatie die hij zelf vond wil hij een boek schrijven.

Burgemeester jeuris heette zijn tegenvoeter hartelijk welkom. Hij zei dat de heer Stooke al voor de tweede keer in Alken was. De eerste keer was wel een toevallige en originele kennismaking: „U wist toen niet waar u landde, u kwam onzacht tegen de vlakte met uw parachute en was onwetend over het feit of u tussen vrienden of vijanden terechtgekomen waart". Het was trouwens hartje nacht en dan is het ook in Alken donker. Een geluk dat Stooke toen de familie Vanderstraeten tegenkwam om hem op de goeie weg te zetten... richting Londen. Ter gelegenheid van zijn tweede bezoek aan het brouwersdorp wilde de burgemeester de dank en erkentelijkheid van de gemeente overbrengen aan hen die het vege lijf veil hadden voor de bevrijding van ht bezette land.

Twee appels

Stooke had intussen ook al vier woorden Nederlands geleerd. „Dames en heren" en „hartelijk dank" bleken verstaanbaar, de rest moest dan maar in kangoeroe-Engels gebeuren. Hij dankte de mensen die hem in de houten barak vonden, de lieve dames die hem bemoederend twee appels gaf. Zo vertelde hij zijn verhaal. „Onze bommenwerper behoorde tot het 416de Squadron, een Australisch squadron in het Engelse Lincolshire. We hadden een opdracht boven Duitsland, in Wuppertal. Maar boven ons doel werden we geraakt door het luchtafweergeschut en twee motoren waren buiten werking. We verloren snel hoogte. In glijvlucht vlo-

gen we over Keulen, en toen moest ik de beslissing nemen: landen of springen.Een noodlanding in de nacht op onbekend gebied was onmogelijk, dus springen maar. Bij mijn weten zijn wij één van de weinig bemanningen die volledig uit een vallend vliegtuig kon ontsnappen. Ik verliet als laatste de bommenwerper".

Op het ogenblik van de crash was Stooke 20 jaar, een snotneus eigenlijk die het bevel voerde over zo'n grote machine, wat een Lancaster bommenwerper toch was. Stooke vertelt verder: „Ik kwam terecht in een wei, en de koe waarnaast ik terechtkwam zal zeker zo verschrikt zijn geweest als ik. Met de hulp van de Alkenaren kwam ik in de richting van Binche, waar de heer Smeyers me verder hielp". Smeyers heeft tenslotte ervoor gezorgd dat Stooke terug in Engeland aankwam.

Een stuk van vliegtuig

Bij dergelijke ontvangsten horen ook geschenken. Burgemeester Jeuris overhandigde Stooke de schotel van de gemeente Alken, en de ouderdomsdeken van de Alkense

Een Australisch piloot, Stooke, kwam na 47 jaar eens kijken waar hij was neergestort. Ook zijn tweede bezoek aan Alken zal hem lang bijblijven. J.Z.

oudstrijders, Jef Huygen had een niet alledaags geschenk: een foto van de brokstukken van de Lancaster van Stooke en een origineel stuk van het vliegtuig, een inlaatklep uit een motor. Daarnaast waren er nog originele documenten uit het vliegtuig, die Stooke ging laten zien aan zijn navigator van toen. De Australische piloot dankte de gemeenschap van

Alken nog voor de gastvrijheid:

„Ik heb wel honderd mensen om hulp gevraagd in mijn tocht door België, en nooit heb ik een weigering gekregen: het begon met Jules en Jef Vanderstraeten en eindigde bij de heer. Smeyers. Nu heb ik de kans: mijn dank te betuigen, iets wat ik 47 jaar geleden niet kon". J.Z.

A NEWSPAPER REPORT ON THE AUTHOR'S RETURN VISIT TO BELGIUM;
'PILOT STOOKE DROPPED IN 1943 FROM THE SKY -
BACK IN ALKEN 47 YEARS AFTER THE CRASH.'

THE AUTHOR AT THE CIVIC RECEPTION IN ALKEN - 1990.

PAOLO AND JEANNE SMEYERS WITH THEIR FAMILY - 1990

PAOLO SMEYERS, "LITTLE" MARIER-CLAIRE, THE AUTHOR, JOE (MARIE CLAIRE'S HUSBAND) AND JOY STOOKE AT ARBRE - 1990

Our visit to Paris included an inspection of Fresnes prison but, thankfully, only from the outside this time. I thank my boyhood friend Jacques Mason, now a Parisien, for his help and guidance.

In Germany, we found Dulag-Luft to be hardly recognisable as most of the old buildings had been demolished. Today it is called Camp King and is an American Transport Depot. Lieutenant Colonel Robert Wentz, U.S. Army and Franz Gajdosch showed us around what was left of this former German Interrogation Centre.

Back in England, Joy and I stayed at the Bromley home of D-Donald's wireless operator Dennis Toohig and his wife Kathleen. Then we drove to ex-Royal Australian Air Force Station, Binbrook, and were allowed to look around its now unoccupied buildings, taking the time to drink one or two ales at 460 Squadron's watering hole, the Marquis of Granby pub. This visit satisfied my determination to return to Binbrook representing my crew, so ensuring that they were numbered amongst the lucky few aircrew who were able to comply with the Squadron's motto, 'Strike and Return'. Our return, however, was 47 years overdue.

460 SQUADRON
ROYAL AUSTRALIAN AIR FORCE

This Squadron flew the greatest number of sorties,
dropped the greatest tonnage of bombs,
suffered the heaviest casualties and
received the most decorations,
of any squadron in the history of the R.A.F.

There were five Australian Squadrons
operating in Bomber Command
during World War 2.

Of those, 460 Squadron alone, lost
over 1000 young Australians in raids
over Germany.

Those men, some still in their teens,
Struck but did not Return.

Lest We Forget.

PEOPLE MENTIONED IN THE TEXT

APPERLEY George and daughter Joy
BALTHAZAR Father Henry
BECKER Oberst/L Otto
BELL Jack
BEST Frank
BROADBENT Colin
'BRUMMY' - boxing friend
BRUYNOGHE Dr Guy
BRUYNOGHE Margot & Yannick
CARR Air Vice Marshall C
CHADWICK Roy
CRAVEN Clarrie
CHURCHILL Jim
CHURCHILL Peter
CONKLIN Norm
de GAULLE Geneviere
DELESTRAINT General
de ZITTER Prospere-Valere
DODD Keith
DOWNEY Dan
EDWARDS Group Captain Hughie
EDRARD Jean-Marie
FROMOND Francine
GANSLER Gestapo Kommissar
GANSLER Wilhelm
GAJDOSH Franz
GARGINI Sergeant E
GIBSON Wing Commander Guy
GIRALT Florentine
GODEAU Father
HANDKE Hauptmann
HARRIS 'Taffy'
HAULTECOEUR Renee
HEWITT Jack
HILTON Jack
HUYGEN Josef
JEURIS Mayor Raymond
JONES Sandy
JURION Ernist
LENT Hauptmann Helmut
McPHAN Pilot R
MALLORY Herbert
MARTIN Wing Commander Chad
MASON Jacques

MASSEY Wally
MEYERS Jack 'Snowshoes'
NICOD General and Madam Emile
NICOD-GENICOD Juliette
NOWLAN 'Rowdy'
NUTTAL Corporal Jim
OFFICER Gus
PARSONS Air Commodor Keith
PHELPER Lou
PRINCE Germaine
RICHTHOFEN 'Red Barron'
RICE Air Commodor
RICHARDSON Alex
ROCHEFOUCAULD Yvonne
ROCHEZ-JURION Ailine
ROCHEZ Maurice & Leon
RUMPLEHARDT Fritz
SANSON Odette Marie & Roy
SCHMIDT Kurt
SCHNAUFER Major Heinz
SHAW Frank
SMEYERS-JURION Alice
SMEYERS Blanche, Franz, Jacky,
SMEYERS Jeanne, John, Paolo
'SMITHY' Geoff Taylor's friend
SMOLDERS Luc
TAYLOR Geoff
TOOHIG Dennis & Kathleen
von STAUFFENBERG Claus
WATSON Jock
WENTZ L/C Robert

OTHER BOOKS PUBLISHED BY:
AUSTRALIAN MILITARY HISTORY PUBLICATIONS
13 VERONICA PLACE, LOFTUS. 2232. AUSTRALIA. 015-284-760

LONE EVADER BY RAAF PILOT TED COATES. (115 SQUADRON)
THE FIRST MAN TO ESCAPE FRANCE ASSISTED ONLY BY LOCALS
AND WITH NO HELP FROM THE 'UNDERGROUND'

MILNE BAY 1942 BY CLIVE BAKER & GREG KNIGHT.
A 500 PAGE ACCOUNT OF THE 1942 BATTLE IN PAPUA.

TRUSCOTT BY JOHN AND CAROL BEASY.
HISTORY OF THE SECRET WEST-AUSTRALIAN AIR BASE.

TORRES STRAIT FORCE BY REG BALL.
DEFENCE OF TORRES STRAIT AREA AND DUTCH NEW GUINEA

COMMANDO DOUBLE BLACK BY ANDIE PIRIE.
THE HISTORY OF THE 2/5th INDEPENDENT 'COMMANDO' COMPANY.

COMMANDO WHITE DIAMOND BY DON ASTILL.
HISTORY OF THE 2/8th INDEPENDENT 'COMMANDO' COMPANY.

DIGGERS SONGS BY WARREN FAHEY.
A BOOK OF 300 SONGS FROM ALL OF AUSTRALIA'S WARS.

THE CLOWES REPORT
GENERAL CLOWES' REPORT ON THE BATTLE OF MILNE BAY.

SHIFTING SAND & SAVAGE JUNGLE BY GEORGE TARLINGTON. A
BREN GUNNER WITH THE 2/2 Bn FROM SYRIA TO KOKODA.

WALKING THE KOKODA TRAIL BY CLIVE BAKER.
MODERN TREK GUIDE TO THE TRAIL AND ITS BATTLE FIELDS.

MANY OTHER TITLES - WRITE FOR A FULL BROCHURE.